T0018150

Read this now, no matter the age of your children, because understanding how to let go as your children age is essential to keeping their hearts secure. When you get this right, they'll listen and believe your insights and input. They'll seek your wisdom! Dr. Smith's principles are excellent and his methods will work.

~Kathy Koch, PhD, Founder, Celebrate
Kids, Inc., and the author of
8 Great Smarts, Start with the Heart,
and *Screens and Teens.*

I have known Roger and Jan for many years and have always appreciated their love for God, their family, and their community. They are caring, authentic, and always available. As I was reading through **Parenting with Influence**, I loved the blend of folksy wisdom, medical insights, and practical application with their own children. This to me is a treasure trove of common sense knowledge gathered over decades of working with people in a wide variety of settings. I commend Roger for taking the time to share with us what he has gleaned.

~Steve Demme, creator of
Math-u-see Curriculum

"*Parenting with Influence* is that wise-but-practical friend you've been looking for."

~Hal and Melanie Young, authors of
No Longer Little and *Raising Real Men*

Parenting with Influence

SHIFTING YOUR PARENTING STYLE
AS YOU AND YOUR CHILD GROW

Roger Smith, MD

WESTBOW
PRESS®
A DIVISION OF THOMAS NELSON
& ZONDERVAN

WestBow Press books may be ordered through booksellers or by contacting:

WestBow Press
A Division of Thomas Nelson & Zondervan
1663 Liberty Drive
Bloomington, IN 47403
www.westbowpress.com
844-714-3454

ISBN: 978-1-6642-6391-8 (sc)
ISBN: 978-1-6642-6392-5 (hc)
ISBN: 978-1-6642-6390-1 (e)

Library of Congress Control Number: 2022907224

Print information available on the last page.

WestBow Press rev. date: 06/09/2022

CONTENTS

INTRODUCTION

Someone's Future Is at Stake

I have spent a large part of my adult life mentoring, shepherding, and caring for teenagers. As a father, doctor, scouting leader, baseball coach, and national speech and debate coach, I have often glimpsed in these young adults enormous potential and ability percolating just below the surface, waiting to burst out. At the same time, I have witnessed some disturbing trends that threaten to snuff the very life and hope out of them. One is the unchecked escalation of teenage rebellion, resentment, angst, and alienation we see sweeping through our culture. Another is our willingness to accept this situation as totally normal—almost as a rite of passage.

The good news is that it doesn't have to be this way. Throughout this book, I will challenge the notion that the teen years exist to rob young people and their parents of the joy of living. You and I will explore together some foundational principles of parenting that can yield results that are happily at odds with the culture when it comes to our expectations.

No, I am not about to suggest that there is a guaranteed formula for achieving parenting success. At the same time, I wholeheartedly believe there are time-tested principles that, when properly applied, will dramatically increase your chance of raising well-adjusted, engaged adults who actually want you to be a part of their lives.

Wouldn't it be great if every new child came with a manual at birth that explains exactly how this child was designed and describes such features as his or her strengths and weaknesses, temperament, interests, and natural giftings? True, very few parents would bother to read such a manual, and most of those would only refer to it when something was not working and needed troubleshooting. But as it is, our children come to us as a mystery that we must solve, at a time when we have little or no experience with children and, certainly, no experience with *this* child.

Maybe it's a difficult child that has led you to this book. If so, may you find within these pages some helpful answers that improve life for both of you. If you are preparing to meet challenges that lie ahead, may you find some useful preventative measures here. In any case, I hope you will find gems of wisdom and principles for parenting that you will pass on to others who are on this journey with you.

The sooner you, as a parent, understand and implement the concepts outlined herein, the easier it will be to depart from patterns you know to be riddled with trouble and instead take a new approach that will produce better results and a more pleasant journey. While it is best to make such a shift while the teen years are still far off, you may be pressed to change paths immediately if you already find yourself in the midst of family upheaval.

Regardless of where you are along the path, the stage of parenting that seems hardest is the one you're currently in. Being a parent is hard, and few parents are getting the necessary training in this crucial, one-shot-at-it process that will have a profound impact on the future. Who knows? The investment you make in learning to be an effective parent could one day result in saved lives, cured disease, significant industry or culture shifts, or simply the spreading of joy and hope.

Your pursuit to learn more about your children and yourself produces an unmeasurable impact, so I commend you for seeking to grow and change. The uncomfortable truth is, parents must do the changing if we expect things to get better with our children. But I think we all can agree with the statement that it is insanity to keep doing the same things and expect different results.

Within these pages, I am bringing all that I am and have to bear on the subject. I am bringing years of training in pediatrics and an accompanying board certification. I am bringing decades of working with youth and youth volunteers in a wide variety of organizations, both secular and Christian. I am bringing years of personal study about parenting and leadership, as well as the influence of my spiritual mentors and my own parents. I am bringing the experience of working with broken young men in an addiction treatment facility, along with many examples of the impact poor parenting had on them.

Finally, I am laying open before you my family and the Smith home, where you will get to see both good and bad examples of parenting while learning that good results can come out of an imperfect effort, and that anything you do to improve your game will indeed have an impact on the final score. Keep in mind that the stories I tell of how my family and others have navigated these waters are purely for the purpose of illustration and are not intended to suggest ours is the only right or good way. It was just our way, but I hope these examples will serve to move your thinking from the theoretical realm to practical living that results in your children truly feeling loved and valued.

I commend you for reading a book that can benefit not only you but also your children and, hopefully, generations to come. Regardless of your feelings about the current state of your family, there is no time like the present to grow.

Old sayings often capsulize profound truth. Here's one I like: "The best time to plant a tree is twenty-five years ago. The second-best time is today." Now is the second-best time for you to change as a parent.

CHAPTER 1

Parenting with Purpose

During my third year of medical school, my wife, Jan, was rushed into emergency surgery to deliver our struggling son. Being a nerdy medical student, I didn't fully understand what was happening, but I changed into scrubs, grabbed my camera, and followed everyone to the operating suite. I was shuffled to a spot out of the way but where I could photograph my own life transition. Photo after photo captured surgeons and instruments, and finally, of a vulnerable infant being handed hastily to another waiting doctor.

In a series of snapshots, the boy turned from blue to pink, from violet to vigorous! The once slimy, blue baby, now clean and wrapped, was placed in my outstretched and trembling arms. I had seen the status of his health transition from "hanging in the balance" to "bouncing baby boy." What I did not see at that moment was the vastness of how my own life had been forever changed.

When children enter the picture, whether through birth, adoption, marriage, or foster care of some kind, life changes. This change, though wonderful, comes with unexpected levels of stress. One of the parents' objectives, then, is to keep that stress from becoming *distress*.

Of course, just introducing change to any degree results in stress. It is a known fact that heart attacks often occur during happy times such as taking a vacation, sending a child off to college, or entering retirement.[1] These greatly anticipated moments generate stress due to sudden change in our routines and expectations, new decisions, and new experiences—all for which we are unprepared. Sounds a lot like parenting a new child!

Although in life there will always be surprise situations that throw us a bit off balance, a few guiding principles will help us stay the course, just as sailors of old set their gaze upon a star or distant object to help them remain on course despite being buffeted by wind and waves. I have done only enough sailing to get myself thoroughly wet, but as a similar experience, I have often driven a tractor across my pasture while spraying herbicides to control weeds. (Whether the use of such chemicals be wicked or wise is beside the point.) To thoroughly cover the pasture with the clear liquid, I must pick a clear point of reference across the field each time I turn around, drive as straight as I can toward it, and remember that point the next time I turn back in that direction. This then becomes the mark by which I measure my progress. Little by little, I work across the field until I arrive at my destination.

Sailors have an advantage in this analogy, for they instantly know whether they have done a good job navigating when they spy landfall and can determine easily if they got off course. However, when spraying my field, I don't yet know if I have done a good job when I pull the tractor into the barn. For the next two to three weeks, I anxiously await the dying of the weeds, and without fail, I find I have missed strips of pasture where the weeds are flourishing. Sometimes I can see what caused me to veer too far to the right or left. But the spraying is done for the season, and I have to deal with it.

Parenting is not like killing weeds—there is no spray or magic potion. There is, however, a process and a goal. What *is* the goal of parenting? This is a real question I ask you to consider. Stop reading and take a few moments to consider your answer. How would you define your goals as a parent?

Eliminating the Need

Many years ago, when I was in college, I took a required course in child development. The professor began his first lecture with an overview of the course before sharing some introductory thoughts on parenting. That day, he gave us a definition of parenting that shocked me. Yet the more I thought about it, the more I found it to be the simple truth:

Parenting is the process of eliminating your child's need for you.

"Wait a minute!" you might say. "All this stress, all these changes, all the lost sleep, and all this reading is just so my kids will no longer need me?"

Exactly!

One day, when your children are grown, you will be gone. At best, they will move out of your home and you will find yourself playing a different role in their lives. Perhaps they will turn to you for advice and counsel. But there is a path one travels to get this point, and it is called *parenting*—eliminating your child's need for you.

If you are not in the process of eliminating your child's need for you, you are on a long and difficult journey that leads to, possibly, a very bad ending. If your children are not fully independent of you before your death, they will find themselves in quite a predicament when that moment arrives. While your departure is a long time off—you hope—your child's need for independence will come sooner than you think.

Most of us with deceased parents wish we could talk to them from time to time. I still find myself thinking, *What would Dad think about this?* or *Why didn't I get that list of phone numbers from Mom?* Though I would like to have my parents available, I am perfectly capable of getting along without them. They helped to eliminate my need for them.

Look at your children now, compared to last year. Have they made progress in lessening their need for you? As you gaze across the pasture of parenthood to find your next point of destination, can you honestly say that you have you covered the appropriate amount of space? In the most recent swath of life, maybe you had to navigate around an obstacle, or maybe your emotional engine ran hot and you had to veer off track to get water and blow off some steam. But the job demands that you get back in the groove, not forgetting the task at hand of progressing toward eliminating your child's need for you.

We often refer to this goal as "maturity," as if it is a destination to which one suddenly arrives. Like growing fruit on a tree, it takes some time. And each step in the process of producing fruit is *so* important to the quality of the final product. Sometimes we fail to see and appreciate the value of some seasons, such as a biting, frigid winter or painfully sweltering summer, but they are all important. And some trees take many years to produce a viable crop.

This reminds me of a mistake I made while in medical school. In the summers, I ran a lawn care company called Medical Student Lawn Service. We had a sandwich-board-type sign that we would set out where we were working to promote our name and slogan: "Watch us operate!" One day, we were operating on the largest yard we had yet acquired, a beautiful four-acre place. We were determined to do a good job for this client.

After our first time mowing his place, the client pulled me aside to talk in private. He told me I had just mowed down his wife's bed of asparagus! I was raised as the son of a grocer and had only seen asparagus in its final stage, never during the growth process. This lady's prized asparagus had looked like weeds to me. Little did I know asparagus does not look like the edible vegetable until it has grown for two to three years. Something I saw as having no value had been in the process of producing an expensive commodity, one that would keep on producing annually if some knucklehead had not mown it down.

We cannot afford to be knucklehead parents who stop our child's growth. We must be able to see the important, valuable things in the lives of our children, and be careful to help them grow. As we go through life with them, like me trying to spray the weeds in my pasture, we must cover as much of life's terrain as we can, diligently watching for signs of progress and remembering that our job is to move ever closer to the point where our children no longer need us.

CHAPTER 2

Finding the Source of Resentment and Rebellion

Our first child showed us just how little we knew about parenting. We thought we knew what we were doing. After all, we both had been raised by pretty good parents. Both of us were college educated, adept at Bible teachings, and had worked with kids of various ages through youth organizations and church. But then we found ourselves sitting in the hall outside our two-year-old son's door, trying to make him stay in his room and sleep there. We tried everything we knew to convince him that this arrangement was right and good, but he was definitely winning the battle of wills. We suspected that this child would likely grow up to be a leader, for either good or bad, because he would not be deterred!

He is the reason we began an intense study of the parent-child relationship, and in this way the old saying became true in our home: "And a little child shall lead them." Many times along our parenting journey, at least early on, we wondered who was leading whom. But the more we learned about leadership, the more we understood that we were, in fact, leading, regardless of how it looked or felt.

When this child approached his teen years, we and others recognized that he indeed had an aptitude for leadership. At first, we just thought he was difficult and hard to handle, but we eventually realized that his strong will and competitive nature were areas of strength, giftings that needed to be developed. It was then we began studying leadership in earnest, determined to help him grow into an effective leader, though we did not know where it would take him.

Most leadership training materials are produced by business leaders with other persons of business in mind. This in no way deterred our pursuit of knowledge, because we were certain the application would come to us as we understood more and more about both leadership principles and our son. To our surprise, we learned many parenting principles along the way because, after all, parenting is leadership.

Too Much of Nothing

One of the more interesting concepts I picked up from our study of leadership is what I have come to call "relationship math." See what you think of this equation:

$$R + R - R = R + R$$

It doesn't take a mathematician to see that this cannot be a true statement, unless $R = 0$. However, it *is* true of relationships, if properly understood. On the right side of the equal sign, the letters stand for **resentment** and **rebellion**. Resentment and rebellion are rampant in our culture to the point that those attitudes are now considered normal and expected in children whether they be tweens, teens, or twenty-somethings. However, it not only doesn't have to be that way, it *shouldn't* be that way.

Though resentment and rebellion in the younger generation are nothing new, these attitudes seem to be running at an all-time high, at least in the United States. Many factors have contributed to their prevalence, but rather than trying to lay the blame on one thing or another, it is more productive to look for solutions. The solution lies, in part, with the equation above.

If resentment and rebellion are present in a home or workplace, they're likely the result of conditions present on the left side of the equation. So what do the three R's in $R + R - R$ stand for? **Rules** and **regulations** without **relationship**. Or better stated, rules and regulations *out of balance with* relationship. Wherever rules and regulations are the main emphasis, taking precedent over relationship, the person subject to those rules and regulations will, over time, come to feel smaller and smaller in value. Maybe even like a "big fat zero."

In the beginning—whether it be childhood, a new job, or learning a new skill—our tolerance for rules and regulations is relatively high, because it is through them that we learn how to function. But our tolerance for the rules fades as our competence increases. Then the rules and regulations become more of a hindrance and source of frustration.

The tale has been told of Thomas Edison's laboratory where he and his team conducted thousands of experiments and made numerous discoveries leading to more than 1,000 patents. When a new employee inquired as to the rules he must observe in the lab, Edison replied, "There are no rules here. We're trying to accomplish something!" That may have been the case in his laboratory, but the world does not usually operate that way and neither should your home. On the other hand, neither should the rules reign supreme.

Tales from the Rodney Files

One of my sons was not very good at following rules, and he taught us the most about keeping rules and regulations in their proper perspective. Because he has a natural propensity for testing the flexibility of any rule, some of our best family stories involve him. Though these experiences were often far from funny at the time, the recalling of tales from the life of Rodney Smith are often a source of laughter at family gatherings. One such event occurred at the local rodeo.

To this day, we don't know the whole truth, but here are the basic facts: My wife was making her way out of the rodeo grounds with the exiting crowd when she spotted her handcuffed, thirteen-year-old son being stuffed into the back of a police car. As in all such stories, there are three sides: Rodney's side, the officer's side, and the truth. Regardless of the details, what we know for certain is that the incident involved an imbalance of rules and regulations with relationship.

Granted, something obviously happened that caused the officer to set his "affections" upon my son. That something had to do with rules and regulations, which the officer was acutely focused on to the exclusion of any knowledge of the person or situation. Neither did he seek to further understand the situation but, rather, jumped to conclusions. Whereupon Rodney became resentful and rebellious, his attitude confirming to the officer what he had presumed about the young man. Thus the situation rapidly devolved into a tangled, emotional mess that had started rather innocently over the incorrect disposal of trash (or so it seems).

The long arm of the law, in this case, had a short fuse. The officer flexed his muscles to "get some respect," because in some way Rodney had flouted his authority. But this very act resulted in further disrespect, all because the rules and regulations were enforced without any attempt at establishing relationship. If the officer had assessed the situation more objectively, he might have seen that my son was clowning around and not meaning to dishonor the officer or disrespect his authority.

Let me pause here for a second, because I never want to imply that a police officer's job is easy or that police should be slow about assessing a situation. I understand that they must assume the worst in any circumstance. Otherwise, they may expose themselves to danger or, by inaction, allow civilians to be put in harm's way. So I don't fault this particular officer for his actions that day. I tell you this story only as an example of how we, as parental authorities, can jump to erroneous conclusions when our relationship with a child is such that we believe the worst in him or her. Thus we are quick to throw the rulebook at the child in anger rather than guiding him or her to live successfully within the boundaries of the rules and regulations.

Pain from the Past

Perhaps you have painful memories of a personal injustice or harsh punishment that was out of proportion to your transgression, and to this day, you have an emotional response when your memory of that incident is brought to the surface. I have a memory of a painful injustice from my childhood involving my dad and one of my brothers.

One night when I was fifteen, long before there was such a thing as a cellular phone, my sister stayed out far past curfew. We hadn't heard from her, and my father became more worried and upset the longer he waited for her to walk through the door. I was scared for my sister, and so was my older brother, who happened to be home from college for the week. He too saw that my dad's concern and disappointment with my sister was turning to anger and then to rage. Then our enraged father decided to go out and look for her.

It was near midnight when my brother stepped in, and his hurt came spilling out. He stopped our dad at the door and, for the first time, I heard about how my father had believed a lie about my brother that a stranger had told him ten years earlier. When my brother was just a lad of nine or ten years old, he was severely punished for something he did not do, and then was punished again for denying it was true. On this night, I heard my twenty-year-old brother, with passion, pain, and tears, retell the story of his childhood injustice as he pleaded with my father to get more information before declaring a guilty verdict in the case of our sister. Ten years had passed since the earlier incident, but the lingering hurt was painfully present in my brother's voice. In that moment, I learned a person could be deeply injured by another—even someone who believed he or she was doing the right and responsible thing—and then carry that pain around inside him.

Even at the age of fifteen, just barely in high school, I knew that although my sister was clearly in the wrong, my father was somehow on the verge of making the situation much worse. Yet by some miracle my brother's plea was heard, and my father regained his composure.

That night, my brother grew to be ten feet tall in my eyes, for he had bravely reopened an old, deep wound and turned his personal pain into someone else's protection. He redeemed an injustice to himself to ensure justice for another. He had the courage to speak up and save my father from an action he would regret.

There is no doubt that unresolved pain can become poison to the soul if the injury that caused it remains unforgiven. If deep-rooted emotional pain looms large in your past, it will affect your parenting—it will either make you a rule-maker or make you hopeless. So where there exists deep, unresolved hurt, find someone to help you forgive, then turn it into something good.

The age-old admonishment "Forgive and forget" is not something we can do or should do. Yes, we remember when someone hurts us or betrays our trust, and we learn something in the process. At the same time, we can forgive the guilty party. That is, we no longer wish for retaliation or recompense, nor do we wish ill to come to them. But from the lessons learned in the process, we can become equipped to handle similar situations in the future.

My brother did just that. The painful memory enabled him to confront a bad situation, cooling rage with reason and preventing further trouble. My hope for you, if you have such pain from your past, is that you will be able to draw upon your experiences to the good of others, especially your children.

If the pain and trauma from your past is negatively affecting your current relationships, it is imperative that you find a counselor to help you work through the painful memories so that you do not reproduce your pain in the lives of those close to you. Often, attempts to correct past traumas on one's own results in overcorrection. A common overcorrection that parents make is making onerous rules for situations that once caused them great pain. This often produces new pain for the child subject to the rules. Thus the rules and regulations meant to prevent trouble become the source of it, creating an atmosphere that puts a strain on the relationship between parent and child.

Does Your Child Feel Loved?

No parent desires to break the spirit of his children with excessive rules and regulations but, instead, wants them to know beyond a shadow of a doubt that love motivates him to set boundaries meant to guide them safely to a good place. Children are enabled to receive correction when they are confident of their parents' acceptance and love. It is *feeling* loved that makes all the difference.

How to Really Love Your Child by Dr. D. Ross Campbell is a book that opened my eyes, empowering me to understand my children and my role as a parent. In his introduction, Campbell writes, "The truth is that most parents really do love their children, but the fact remains that most children do not *feel* loved."[1] It is imperative that we learn how to clearly communicate love to our children in ways they can feel it.

All of my children are adults now. We are proud of all four, three boys and a girl. Our daughter especially helped us grow in the area of communicating love. In her early adult years, she became very defensive during simple conversations around the dinner table when any philosophical, political, or social issue came up. Though I don't remember any particular issue, the atmosphere grew tense during these conversations. My wife and I realized that something was wrong, but we made a pact that we would not react emotionally to anything our daughter might say or reveal to us. We remained interested and open, and little by little, she tested the waters by sharing ideas she was exploring on a variety of topics, ideas she knew differed from our own.

In each conversation, we affirmed what we agreed with; on positions where we differed, we pointed to other people we respected who agreed with her. She would then venture a bit further on some difficult issues, testing us in two ways. First, she tested our commitment to and understanding of our own beliefs. But secondly, and more importantly, she would test whether our love for her was greater than our differences. When it became clear to us what was happening, I laid it on the line: "Emily, you cannot say, think, or do anything that is going to decrease my love for you or my acceptance of you."

Although it took a few months for her to fully believe and trust us in this, we now enjoy a profoundly close relationship with the very child with whom we have the greatest differences. That's because we really know and truly value one another. We have worked hard to communicate to her the value we place on the relationship. Where our daughter once felt the fear of rejection, she now feels our love. Fear is the opposite of love. Perfect love—or in this case, determined love—"casts out fear."[2]

People often speak of the virtues of unconditional love. But I must ask the question, "Is there any other kind?" Loving those who love you back is easy. What's exciting is seeing someone who thinks you *will not* love them come to realize that you *do*. This changes everything in the relationship.

Through years of observing others and through my own experience, I can confidently say this:

Relationship is the key to preventing or resolving resentment and rebellion.

Where the relationship is fragile, frustrating, or fearful, bad things add up and family turmoil prevails. Where love is clearly expressed and felt, trust is the order of the day, leading to more productive and satisfying results for all.

Does your child *feel* loved?

CHAPTER 3

Where Do Rules Fit In?

For ten years, I volunteered at a local rehabilitation center where I taught a weekly class on relationships. Most people who need to rehab from drug- or alcohol-related problems have a history of making relationship mistakes. In addition, they usually have had poor training in, or poor examples of, managing relationships. It's often hard to tell which came first. Did chemical dependence lead to the individual's problems with relationships, or did relationship problems lead to an escape that became chemical dependence? Both have been true, but suffice it to say, I have heard from a lot of people with relationship problems.

The men I worked with ranged in age from eighteen to seventy. Whenever I discussed rules and regulations with them, I was continually amazed by their responses. Though I didn't keep an actual count, nearly all said that rules and regulations had created problems in their lives. About two-thirds of the participants said their parents were overly strict and harsh, while the other third said that having *no* rules in their upbringing led to the problems that had brought them to rehab. I heard the unmistakable anger in the voices of those men raised by harsh, rules-focused parents, but what haunts me to this day is the look in the eyes of those who said their parents were the exact opposite.

The ones who grew up with no rules were usually the quietest and the saddest of the group. When asked why their parents' (or caretakers') permissiveness was a problem, they universally said it was a sign to them that no one really cared. No one was willing to be inconvenienced by setting or enforcing a standard of behavior, and that sent a clear message to these lost boys that they were simply not worth the trouble. Some told me the lack of rules led them to believe that their actions had no real significance or consequence, and therefore they felt unrestrained to make choices they *knew* were wrong, but what did it really matter? They were convinced they were worthless to those who were supposed to love and protect them, so they lived as though their lives had no value or meaning. Thus began a lifelong pattern of self-destructive thinking and behavior.

In many of these cases, I sensed that the parents sincerely loved their children, putting the child's needs before their own, but were following misguided child-rearing advice. In other cases, it seemed the parents were afraid of being rejected by the child and therefore sought to create a world of opportunity where pleasures and excitement were used almost as a lure to win the child's affection.

In many of these cases where essentially no rules existed, the children responded far differently than the parents had anticipated. One childish thought or action led to another, more aggressive or more grievous one, eventually culminating in complete lawlessness, jail time, or seven months in a rehab center. The parents' attempt to provide their child a "happy life" resulted in a sad, bad, and mad adult.

Though I do believe that we, as parents, are responsible in many ways for how our children turn out, I don't share these stories as evidence that parents are solely to blame for the decisions and actions of their children. I share these stories to challenge you to sharpen your own decision-making skills.

There's a comical saying that goes, "A wise man learns from his mistakes, but a genius learns from the mistakes of others." Though we always need to be wise, it is essential that we become geniuses by this definition. For in parenting, by the time we've gained enough insight to learn from our own mistakes, we have plowed such deep rows in the lives of our children that the landscape of their futures has been forever altered.

No parent starts out with a plan to mark their children with emotional, psychological, or physical scars. Many of us just veer off course somewhere along the way and begin thinking more about our own needs and insecurities rather than focusing on the horizon and keeping our sights set on that point of destination to which we want to take our child. Sometimes this happens through no fault of our own. Death, financial catastrophe, illness, or other stressors outside our control grab our time and attention or even drain our will to win in life. When loss of will or loss of perspective sidetracks us as parents, our children don't always understand what's happening. They only know how it makes them feel.

Where to Find Support and Useful Guidance

Whatever our circumstances, we must be careful to avoid trying to meet our emotional needs through our children. Though it is right and good for us to take joy in our children, there must be another adult in our lives who helps meet our emotional and spiritual needs so that we are free to pour into our children. If we are dependent on our children for soothing the wounds in our own lives, we will be unable to lead effectively because, in effect, we are asking *them* to lead *us*.

Find a friend, a mentor, an advisor who has little to gain from sharing in your troubles yet is willing to walk through life's traumas with you. Hopefully, that person is your spouse, but sometimes he or she is not enough because you're both working at less than emotional capacity due to the same stressors. Consider talking with a paid counselor or a church friend or neighbor. Find a person who is willing to know you, understand you, and confront you when necessary. Make it someone older, if possible; time and experience do give a person deeper perspective on life issues.

Your trusted "advisor" may be a book; it might be the only immediate, non-condemning source of honest insight available to you. Often, however, a book is not enough because we all need the physical reassurance of a real person. So keep your eyes open for the right individual.

Regarding books, don't let finances keep you from getting the input and guidance you need. I remember the dark days of my residency when we lived a thousand miles from friends and family. We had no extra money and two small children. It would be an understatement to say that our oldest child was strong-willed. My wife was fatigued, frustrated, and frightened as she tried to teach that boy to obey without breaking his spirit or losing her mind. I knew the situation was serious when she called me at the hospital one day and screamed over the phone, "Either he sees a psychiatrist or I do!"

For weeks, I had known my wife was crying, praying, and worrying over the endless challenges presented by our three-year-old. He wouldn't stay in his bed or sleep in his room, and he would climb on top of the refrigerator! He would not take no for an answer, yet "no" was often the only answer we could get out of him! He frequently acted as if we were his archenemies—unless we were in public, where he became an absolute angel, making us look foolish when we dared to mention that he was a holy terror. We began early to recognize a future leader in this three-year-old body, but this didn't make us feel much better about our situation. For all we knew, this future Napoleon was going to lead a whole band of people over some cultural or spiritual cliff.

My wife, Jan, has always been resourceful, but now she was also desperate. At the time, we lived in Lexington, Kentucky, not far from a decent bookstore. Although our store was nice, this was before the days when bookstores began offering coffee shops and lounge areas for customers to sit and peruse the books. But a lack of seating was no deterrent for Jan! She dropped our kids off with a "volunteer" babysitter, who it seems was willing to trade her services for free clothing repairs. Then Jan made her way to Joseph-Beth Booksellers five blocks from our house to seek wisdom from James Dobson's book *The Strong-Willed Child*. She found a bare spot on the floor at the end of a row of shelves and sat down to read. The floor was just fine with Jan, partly because she didn't want the other customers to see her desperate tears as she scoured the pages, looking for help. We never paid for that book, but it tossed a lifeline of hope to my wife who was drowning in fear of failure. While we never found the magic bullet to solve all our parenting issues, Dr. Dobson's book provided enough hope and comfort to help us hang on until our son (and we) grew a bit and the battle lines shifted.

Remember, you don't have to buy a book to get help from it,

although it is much more convenient to own a copy. Check for sales and discounts through your favorite online retailer or local bookstore. PaperbackSwap.com is a great place to pick up books for the price of postage. And don't forget your public library. Thanks to Benjamin Franklin, who founded the first public library in 1731, today there are more lending libraries in the U.S. than McDonald's and Subway franchises combined.

A word of warning: Don't overvalue an author's academic credentials when selecting a book of parenting advice. It's not the letters behind the name or degrees on a wall that make an author an expert. Make sure he or she has lived through to completion what he or she espouses as "the way." Don't take advice on raising teens from someone who has only toddlers at home.

There are, of course, a few reliable, even brilliant, authors who don't meet this stipulation. One I recommend is Dr. Kathy Koch, who has made a career of studying teenagers but has no children of her own. Her insights and wisdom go far beyond what one would expect from someone who has not personally endured the struggles and adjustments involved in parenting a teen. Dr. Koch's books and resources are trustworthy, helpful, and filled with pearls of wisdom. As I said, there are exceptions to the principle of seeking out only experienced parent-authors, but not many.

Wherever you go for help, avoid giving in to the victim mentality that resorts to self-pity, hopelessness, or apathy. The biblical book of Proverbs suggests that we must seek out wisdom as one would seek buried treasure —with dogged determination to find it.

The Benefit of Clear Boundaries

Our children need us to set clear boundaries and manage the rules and regulations necessary to train and comfort them. Yes, you read that right. Rules both train *and* comfort. Rules for acceptable behavior train children to know what is right and good before they are able to understand the why behind it. Rules keep the ball from breaking the lamp and the bike from rusting in the rain. They prevent the baby from getting a concussion, the toddler from burning his hand. They keep the preteen from developing bad habits and teens from becoming self-centered. These are example of how rules help to train a child, but how do they produce comfort?

Boundaries in life provide a place of comfort and a place for freedom. When Christopher Columbus set out to find a path to India by sailing westward, he recruited brave and bold sailors who, in their day, were some of the strongest and hardiest men on land or sea. There were no wimps on the crews of ships sailing into open, uncharted waters where dangers real and imagined lurked beneath the wind and waves, not to mention the ever-present threat of pirates. Only courageous men with adventuresome spirits would sail with Columbus into the unknown.

Yet after many days, these same brave men became frightened to the point of desperation. Fear had overtaken them to the point that they were threatening to mutiny unless the captain turned the ship around. What could unnerve able-bodied seamen to this degree? Unclear boundaries. Even salty sea dogs knew that life had rules and boundaries, and as long as they remained within those boundaries, they knew what to expect and were prepared to deal with it. In their minds, the world had an edge, a boundary, beyond which all was lost. When they became uncertain where they stood in relation to that boundary, their thoughts and behaviors became difficult to control.

Our children need us to define for them the boundaries of expected behavior, thoughts, and character as clearly as possible and review those boundaries as often as needed for them to remember. In other words, we should teach the lesson before giving the test when it comes to rules. Two examples come to mind that demonstrate how helpful it is to give the lesson before the test.

My friend Rick from Virginia tells of a time when his wife would become overwhelmed by a trip to the grocery. It wasn't that she feared crowds or driving or shopping decisions. The problem was the seven children she took to the store with her and the other seven she left at home! Maybe I exaggerate. I think they have only thirteen kids. Regardless, she had a lot to manage at the grocery beyond deciding what to put into the cart. Kids can easily get out of control in a supermarket, especially on the cereal aisle where every box has some gadget or gimmick "free inside" to entice a child. Long, straight aisles are excellent for racing or playing catch. Product displays make great places to hide from Mom so she can take a break from shopping to play hide-and-seek while pushing a cart containing two small children and fifty pounds of groceries. And then there is the dreaded checkout line, with shelves of candy packaged in just the right size to fit in the palm of a seven-year-old.

When Rick learned of the trauma of buying groceries with several kids in tow, he responded by creating some rules of behavior for his children, such as staying within an arm's reach of the cart, allowing the child to point out things they like without asking for it, and greeting other customers with eye contact and a smile. After reviewing the rules with all the involved parties, Rick took his kids to the store to practice. They didn't buy anything but slowly went through the store, walking every aisle while greeting the other customers pleasantly. He observed their actions and guided them toward successfully implementing the new rules. This forever changed the family's trips to the market, all because Rick set some boundaries and taught the lessons with practice before the kids were put to the test with a regular shopping trip.

In a similar way, my wife will talk to our children before taking them out in public, because that's where the stakes are highest. We might scream at those little devils at home, but in public, everyone prefers interacting with a band of happy little angels. Occasionally, we sneak them one of our "mean" faces while no one is looking so the kids will know we mean business.

The first time I heard Jan give one of her "pep talks," I thought it was ingenious. She would clearly describe to the children where we were going, what it was like in those buildings, the types of distractions they might encounter, and more importantly, what kind of behavior would make her proud and honor their father and mother. She prepared them to succeed and rejoiced when they did. This approach was especially helpful in new situations, like visiting me at the hospital when I was working or going with her to an obstetrics appointment. What made all the difference was setting boundaries with the goal of succeeding instead of looking for an opportunity to punish.

Granted, we have had plenty of opportunities to dole out punishment;

we don't have to prime that pump. But we have learned that children usually want to be found pleasing to their parents once they have experienced the sensation. Kids just need to clearly understand what is expected of them. As long as the parents' expectations are realistic, rules and regulations can help you maintain the peace while providing training and comfort for your child. Just remember to balance the rules with a loving relationship.

A proper balance of rules and relationship creates an environment where the child can clearly know the acceptance and guidance of parents who sincerely love him. It takes tremendous wisdom for you to create the proper balance for the stage your child is in and to adjust the balance as the child grows. The shifting of the balance of rules and relationship is the underlying principle for this book, and the next chapter will lay further foundational principles that will help you move beyond the years of control to the years of significant influence.

CHAPTER 4

Managing by Rules: A House of Cards

In 2009, I got a lesson in rules and regulations in a up close and personal way. I sold my private medical practice and took a job with a medical clinic that is funded by the federal government to render healthcare to poorly served areas. With the federal funding came many rules and regulations about how things were to be done. When I went to work, I noticed a general lack of motivation among the staff. I also noticed signage throughout the office that announced what could and could not be done.

There were signs about how to wash your hands and when to take off gloves. There were volumes of binders containing hundreds of pages of regulations that would cause the staff to smirk when I asked about them. As I looked through the binders and examined the signs, I found there were good ideas and motives behind each. Yet the environment they created did not motivate the staff to comply unless a superior or inspector was watching them. The rules and not the reasons behind them had become the focus in the facility.

Immediately, I felt rebellion rising up in me. I wasn't trained in government regulation, so I began boldly taking down signs and stowing binders full of regulations. The staff would often respond with alarmed facial expressions, so I then began sneaking around when they weren't looking to perform my ritual cleansing. But the list of rules could not be simply removed; they had to be replaced. So I replaced them with a single rule: "Whatever is the right thing to do for the patient is the right thing to do."

More than ten years later, I am still appealing to the integrity of the staff to use their moral compass to decide what is best for the patient rather than fall back on some rule or policy. Worker morale and employee satisfaction has improved over the years, and the rules have slowly become less of an emphasis. The rules have now taken their proper place—confirming whether the staff members have made day-to-day good decisions.

Notice that the rules never went away. I just shifted the focus to the internal rulebook that every employee carries as part of the fabric of their character. When rules and regulations reigned supreme, staff members weren't allowed to be guided by their character, and the rules did not produce in them the character needed to do their jobs. You see, rules and regulations don't produce character, whether in employees or in children. Rules only work to manage external behavior and not the heart.

The Emerging Will, or Who's the Boss?

As children physically mature, so many things are happening beneath the surface, completely unseen to us. It's like a duck on the water, gliding along without visible effort while just beneath the surface he's paddling like crazy. So it is in the mind, emotions, and physical chemistry of a teen. Their minds have newly discovered an ability to doubt, question, or demand more information for understanding. Emotions have become heightened to the point of being able to display marked tenderness and uncontrolled rage almost simultaneously. And the new bumps and bulges on their bodies both impress and embarrass them. It's no wonder teens can seem moody, irritable, even antisocial. The duck inside them is paddling like crazy, and all we want to do is drown the duck! Putting it out of its misery (and ours) often seems like the humane thing to do for all concerned.

But the teenage years are not where the problems begin. The root problem begins several years earlier when children are going through more "innocent" stages. Parents usually don't perceive the developing issue until it becomes more blatant, more in-your-face, as in teenage rebellion or back talk. The good news is that the root problem is identifiable, and whether your children are preschool age or high school age, there are very real, achievable changes you can make now for the good of your family.

Consider the graph in figure 1. Notice that while the child's age progresses from left to right on the graph, there are no exact time markings for when these events are scheduled to happen. Just as toddlers do not all start walking or talking at the same time, adolescence unfolds at a different pace for every young person.

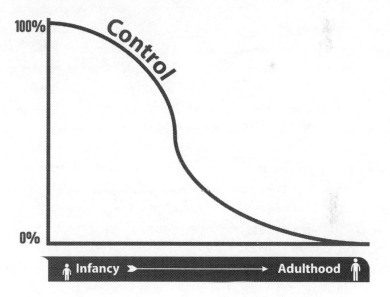

In the beginning, we parents have the most control we will ever exert over our children. The graph depicts the amount of control we have at the beginning to be near 100 percent. We give them what we want them to eat. We select their clothing, decide who holds them, choose the color of their cup, and so on. But over time, we slowly begin to cede a measure of control—willingly or otherwise—to these tiny individuals who look like us. Soon after learning to walk, children begin to express wants and desires that are opposed to their parents' wishes. This struggle, often referred to as "the terrible twos," is one the parents still have the ability to win—most of the time. We can still put food in front of them, but they will decide for themselves whether to ingest it or paint the walls with it. They begin to resist getting into the bath and then resist getting out. Soon, they want to choose for themselves what to wear, or at least refuse to take off their new rubber boots when it's time for bed. As their ability to think, desire, choose, express, and pursue increases, we progressively lose the ability to control them.

To hear most parents talk about their child's emerging will, an alien observer from another world might think this process is dangerous, wicked, and unwise. Or at the very least, undesirable. But once we step back from the current battles with our kids and consider the parenting process objectively, we must recognize and accept that this kind of growth is what we've been aiming for all along! We *want* our children to grow up and cut themselves loose from our apron strings. It's the only way they will ever become self-determining adults with the unassailable character qualities we said we wanted for them before they were born.

We need to see parenting for what it is: *the process of eliminating our children's need for us.* It's all about the transfer of control from parent to child—moving our kids from "parental control" to self-control. When done right, the process is marked by a slow but steady shifting of power through the years, a transition that should be nearing completion by the time the child is old enough to apply for a driver's permit.

If we can keep our eyes on the prize of developing a wise, responsible young adult, our loss of control can be a welcomed process that energizes both parent and child. Undoubtedly, you will make mistakes during this process, but maybe you can learn from my mistakes to avoid making similar ones yourself.

I have a painful memory of a mistake I made with a thirteen-year-old son in 2001, when my eyes were opened to the lie I had believed about how much I could control. Our family had begun participating in competitive speech and debate in order to help our children develop qualities of leadership. Leadership was one of our family's core values, and leaders must be able to communicate, or else they are not able to lead. Competitive speech and debate was one of the tools we chose to use in developing communication skills, and it was working wonderfully with our two oldest children.

On this particular occasion, we had traveled as a family to California to attend a training conference where teenagers' speeches would be critiqued and coaches would help train students in the elements of effective public speaking. The evening before our thirteen-year-old son was to give his speech at the conference, I asked him to practice it with me before he went to bed. "Asking" him to practice was what I thought I was doing, but in reality, I was "telling" him to practice it. That's when the parenting lesson began for me.

We were in the home of a family that had agreed to host us for the weeklong conference. Our elderly hosts saw quickly what was about to happen. Shortly after my son set his jaw and announced, "I don't want to practice," they excused themselves, announcing they were headed to bed. The struggle for control was underway between father and son, and our hosts knew it was going to get ugly. The problem was, I didn't know it. After all, I thought, I've got this under control.

For the next hour, I put pressure on my son in every way I knew, short of punching him in the mouth, and I even considered doing that when he repeatedly told me, "I'm not doing that speech tonight!" I tried logic. I tried staring. I tried guilt. I tried threats. Then I declared that I would stay up all the night until I heard him give that speech. But he was unmoved and even seemed to take pleasure in the fact that he could keep me from sleeping simply by keeping quiet.

My son was in control, and I was not managing it well.

I had begun with noble goals of helping my son develop leadership skills and effective communication, but these goals had gotten lost in a battle of wills. Practices and techniques that had worked well with my older children somehow were not working so well with this child.

After a one-hour standoff, I had to admit that my son was in control. Despite my frustration and intense effort, my son had me in checkmate. Nothing I could do would result in him giving a speech that night. What I feared was that my relationship with this child was forever changed, and it was. It was then I began to understand that what had gone right with my older children had happened largely by chance. As it turned out, I was not an all-wise parent.

Because of many differences in our relationships with the older children and their different personalities, I hadn't noticed that they had begun to take control of their own lives. It didn't *feel* like I was losing control until the third child refused to practice his stupid speech and then took such great pleasure in showing me that I was not able to make him do it.

Today, Jan and I find great pleasure in our relationships with that child who did eventually learn to give those ten-minute speeches. In fact, he now makes his living giving ten-minute sales presentations and attributes much of his success to those painful speech competitions. But more important than that, we find pleasure in the trusting, respectful relationship that was fostered during those years when we could have instead tried to manage by exerting greater control, which would have produced only burned bridges. I also take some joy in the fact that he now has a headstrong daughter much like himself, and as she grows, I will love watching him navigate his relationship with her. It's payback, baby!

Resentment and Rebellion

Face it, parents, you have control of your children for a very brief period in their infancy, but once they begin walking and talking, that control begins to erode. The most troubling time for many parents is during that period when their control is rapidly and irrevocably diminishing. But if you will acknowledge the necessity of this transaction and prepare for it, you can find the process of transferring control to your child to be rewarding. If done well, your relationship with the child will deepen, and both parent and child will flourish. If done poorly, all will struggle.

As parents sense the rising inability to control an aspect of their child's life, the natural response is to try harder. So they impose more rules with harsher penalties and enforce them with angry, loud voices. Yet trying to regain control during this important stage of childhood development serves only to produce some undesirable results.

We must remember that, ultimately, we *want* our children to have control of their own lives. We want them to develop character, autonomy, and ownership of personal responsibility that will bring honor both to them and to us. In other words, losing our control over them is not only natural and normal—it's desirable!

Heavy-handed attempts on our part to resist or reverse this process will result in resentment and rebellion. When parents complain that their child is rebellious, quite often it's a sign the parents are battling to exert control when a better action is needed.

Remember the relationship math, R + R − R = R + R? *Rules and regulations without relationship lead to resentment and rebellion.* The sad truth is that the relationship between parent and child can be damaged when the parent insists on regaining control via an overdependence on rules, and this damage is often difficult to repair. The path I was on with my third child was leading to resentment and rebellion as a lifestyle. I thank God that my eyes were opened to the process before too much damage was done.

Rules and regulation alone do not produce the character we desire in our children. And if overused, they will lead to angry or apathy in the family's relationships. In much the same way I transitioned the medical clinic away from a policy-driven environment that discouraged and frustrated staff to a more individually empowered approach utilizing each worker's moral compass, we need to put household rules and regulations in their proper place so that our children are empowered to grow in character by taking on responsibility and exercising self-control.

The speech standoff between my teenage son and me got resolved, not because I won, but because I found myself looking across the table into the eyes of a young man who knew he had me in checkmate, and I realized there was absolutely no way for me to win. At that moment, many things came into focus as I dialed back my emotional determination to "win" this battle with my son.

Why did I ask Rodney to practice his speech anyway? Was it to help him feel successful and prepared, or was it for me to look good as a parent? Could I have started with a good motive but then switched to a less-noble motive when my offer met with resistance? And if Rodney won this conflict, did that automatically mean I lost? What was I trying to accomplish in this whole ordeal?

"Rodney," I said, "I can't make you practice the speech. My goal was to help you be prepared for tomorrow, but I now understand that you are as prepared as you want to be. I'm okay with that. I was wrong to draw battle lines on this because it's your presentation, not mine. I respect the fact that you stood up for yourself. When you think the speech needs some more work, I'll try to be available to help. I'll see you in the morning. Hope you can get some sleep." With that, I quietly went to bed and encouraged him to do the same.

My instinct, though, was to draw a proverbial line in the sand when I felt challenged. That approach would not have accomplished what I wanted for my son even if I could have made him practice the speech. What I wanted was for Rodney to feel successful, and that would never have happened if I resorted to rules or punishment to make him submit in this one thing. The battle was not really about practicing a speech; it was about the pursuit of excellence. And I would create a desire for excellence in my son not by regulation but, rather, by inspiration.

Rodney had been taking control of the reins of his life, leaving me with less control. Though it was painful, I fondly remember it as a time when I was forced to make a better choice in the relationship with my son—a choice to inspire rather than control.

Turmoil in your family can sometimes be avoided or prevented when the use of rules and regulations is kept in its proper place. Over time, your reliance on control must diminish, and the use of influence in the relationship with your child must rise. This path of parenting is rooted in the hard work of relationship, which is the subject of the next chapter.

CHAPTER 5

The Parental Shift:
The Key to Sanity for All

Influence is the key to completing the parenting journey successfully. Influence is the quality that makes one person intently listen to another. A simple definition might be "the ability to change or affect another person without using direct force or authority."

So what gives parents influence with their children? Is it the parents' position within the family hierarchy? Is it their ongoing ability—and willingness—to provide for their children's needs? What about setting a consistent example of moral excellence? Or is consistency less important than a demonstrated competence in maintaining the home? There is no single component that makes a parent influential with his or her children. Instead, it is a combination of actions and attitudes rooted in the character of the parent and in the relationship that has been fostered with the child.

Think for a moment about the people in your life who have influenced you greatly in a good way. How would you describe your relationship with them? Most of us would respond with words like "genuine," "open," "accepting," "approachable," or something similar. Whatever descriptive words and phrases come to your mind, they will be positive and express a sense of closeness because influence is based on a relationship. The closer the relationship between two people, the more influence one will have with the other.

But when parents try to use control as the primary means of relating to an older child, it is clear what the future holds for this relationship. A controlling environment will only result in dissention, arguments, accusations, disrespect, and disconnection.

A better path toward having influence with your child—through the teen years and beyond—is investing in your influence. "Investing" is the proper term for developing this kind of a relationship because before you can draw on influence to affect your child, you must make significant relationship deposits. This works best if you make a lot of these deposits in the child's early years so you both benefit from the growth of your investment over time. That said, if you're reading this book and have already missed out on opportunities the early years afforded you, be encouraged that it is never too late to begin building a deep, rich, lifelong relationship with your child.

Children are unbelievably forgiving. They want to know the love, acceptance, and approval of their parents. If you currently have a hostile or distant relationship with your child, just know that it may take time to regain his or her trust, but deep inside your child wants it to be good between the two of you. A determined effort on your part is the key to building a bridge of trust that will allow the relationship to heal and grow.

> *It's never too late to build a deep, rich relationship with your child.*

Several years ago, I attended a real estate investment seminar where a presenter spoke about dealing with bankers and loan officers for transactions. He made it clear that most people are intimidated or even frightened by banks and the financial industry as a whole. To help the audience overcome this fear, the speaker encouraged us to have the mindset that we, the customers, should feel like the ones in power, or at least on equal footing with the suits at the bank. He said, "I'll tell you how to get them to call you 'sir.' Either you owe them a million dollars or get them to owe you a million dollars." He wasn't talking about the value of what had been borrowed or loaned but, rather, the intrinsic value of the human transactions. The more transactions that are handled well, the more respect is attached to each one. The more respect there is, the more influence.

When my wife goes to the bank, she is referred to as "Ms. Jan." I assure you, this has nothing to do with a million dollars. Rather, she is treated with respect because for many years, we have engaged in a series of transactions with the bank that threatened neither them nor us. More importantly, our four little towheaded children went with her to conduct these transactions. We had ventured into the laundromat business, among other things, which resulted in regular trips to the bank with fifty-pound bags of quarters and wads of small bills from the change machine. These kinds of deposits set Jan apart from the usual customers who walked in with a few checks in hand. You might think the tellers would dread seeing her come in with our cumbersome deposits, yet her visits seemed to break the monotony. Certainly, having four kids invade your workspace will shake things up a bit!

Though Jan is a highly social person and loves to chat with people, chatting with tellers while they're counting money is not a good fit. It wasn't long before Jan decided there was a better use of her time. Rather than standing by quietly watching someone count money, she began dropping off a fifteen- or sixteen-year-old to make the deposit while she ran another errand. This became standard procedure, and soon, all the bank tellers soon knew our kids by name. With great interest, they watched each of "those Smith kids" grow up, handle the family business transactions, and ultimately, move on to run their own businesses.

In one way, involving our children in these trips to the bank was just the business of getting family stuff done. But these bank visits also represented intentional "deposits" in our relationships with the children where we invested in their sense of the value we place on them.

Take Time to Make Time

In our frantic efforts to manage daily life, barking orders and directing traffic can begin to dominate our parent-child interactions without our realizing it. In this way, we transfer our stress onto the children. And they feel it so acutely, often believing they are being blamed as the cause of their parents' stress.

It's a sad situation when our hectic, overfull schedules cause our children to feel accused. Do you see how easily a child's world is rocked in this situation? The kids feel falsely accused, while their parents are so focused on their to-do list that they fail to sense the need to reassure and comfort their children. Now everyone's emotions are all astir over nothing more than a busy schedule. We must stop the household rat race long enough to communicate value to our children in a way that they can hear it deep in their souls.

Remember the weak spot in the equation $R + R - R = R + R$ is the third R, which represents a relationship that is assigned less value than compliance with the rules and regulations. Attempting to control our children with rules and regulations while undervaluing relationship leads to resentment and rebellion. When we, as parents, get weary, frustrated, fearful, or distracted, our instinct is to try fast-tracking solutions by accentuating the rules rather than taking time to work on the relationship. When we do this, we fuel rebellion in our kids of all ages, but especially teens. They may look like little adults, but the emotional maturity of teenagers is typically not established enough to handle threats and accusations from their parents, from whom they would much rather hear, "I am proud of you."

If you still have some time before your children reach their teen years, you have time to prepare, to implement what you learn in these pages. But if you are already in the midst of the fray, you may need to make some serious adjustments fast. The stakes are high, but you're not the one at risk; your child is.

Your teen is worth the effort it will take to shift your parenting approach to a more effective style, to learn a new way of thinking that will transform your actions and, eventually, your reactions. This is not about being soft or wimpy as a parent. In fact, it will take courage for you to change. It will take strength for you to choose to speak to your teen respectfully. It will take boldness to be gentle. And it will take determination to break down the walls of resistance that have already been built.

I think we can agree that some fights are not worth the effort, but the battle for a healthy relationship with your child is worth giving your final breath. Few things you ever do will last beyond your death, but the legacy of your influence on the life of your child certainly will. I can't stress enough the importance of doing this well.

Relationship: The Source of Influence

So why is the relationship with your child the key to your success as a parent? Because relationship is the source of influence. In the previous chapter, we took our first look at a graph depicting how parental control naturally declines as our children age. However, the graph showed only the "bad" news. There is more to the story, but it will require you to invest in the relationship.

Figure 2 is the same graph but with a second curve showing the potential growth of influence occurring even as we lose control naturally.

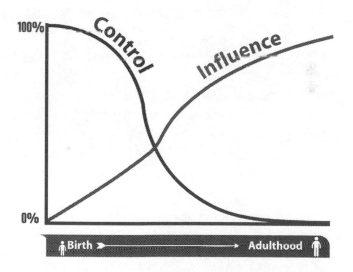

By investing in the kind of relationship that builds influence, we can make a positive impact in the lives of our children both now and continuing into adulthood. If we will shift our parenting emphasis from exerting control to building influence, then we can enjoy the blessing of a relationship that both parent and child find pleasant now and in the future.

This "parental shift" is the underlying principle of this book. As we have seen, ongoing attempts to control or manipulate children beyond the elementary years will likely alienate them from their parents. If over time, however, you will make the shift from an emphasis on control to a mindset of influence, you can rebuild and reinforce bridges between you and your child that will stand well beyond the teen years.

People are driven to read parenting books for a variety of reasons, but generally it's with the aim of making things better at home for both the parent and child. But the reality is, the benefits of strengthening the parent-child relationship overflow from the family and home and extend to friends, neighbors, coworkers, and strangers our children will encounter in life. Unfortunately, we hear more often about the overflow effect involving poor family dynamics. Unresolved discord in families produces negative results that extend beyond the home and are sometimes so severe as to make the evening news. School shootings, vandalism, bullying, crime, disrespect for authority, and other such manifestations are not always the result of poor parenting, but there is often a strong association.

If many poor life decisions can be traced to a dysfunctional home life, we should be heartened to know that the opposite is also true. Repeatedly, studies have shown that a wholesome character in teens and emerging adults is most strongly predicted by a good relationship with at least one of the parents.

The Gen2 Survey, conducted in 2014 among a diverse group of nearly 10,000 young adults between the ages of 18 and 38, confirmed the impact that a healthy relationship with a parent has on a young person's developing character. The study revealed a positive correlation between this relationship and the child's quality of life as an adult as measured in such key areas as their level of civic or community involvement, carrying on their parents' values or faith, and their overall satisfaction with life as an adult.[1] This should further encourage us that the work required to improve our parent-child relationships is not undertaken in vain. These relationships make a vital difference in our ability to pass on important character qualities and life values.

Parenting Is an Uphill Climb—
but It's Worth the Effort

Parenting in many ways parallels what I've experienced hiking mountain trails. The effort it takes to reach the summit of a peak can be physically and emotionally exhausting, evoking thoughts of *Why did I choose to do this? Surely, there's a less strenuous adventure I could have undertaken with my life—one with fewer pitfalls and a greater chance of succeeding.*

In parenting as in climbing, the difficulty of the path can make one feel all alone on the journey. The feeling that no one else knows your struggles, that no one else can relate, creeps into the mind as you fight off pain, fatigue, and fear of failure. Because of this, it's always easier to keep going when you have a traveling buddy. Just like having a hiking buddy helps me not to lose hope on the steep part of the trail, leaning on a spouse, a friend, or a mentor can help keep us from losing hope in the parenting journey.

As you seek to build the kind of trust relationship with your child that is characterized by open communication, it can feel much like climbing a mountain trail. It takes serious effort, and sometimes you will stumble, possibly causing injury to the one next to you as you fall. Fortunately, most injuries are not fatal. In fact, the relationship is strengthened by getting up, repairing the damage, and keeping going. You must apologize when the mistake is yours, ask for and accept forgiveness, then put it behind you as a trail memory to remind you of the progress you've made in the relationship. With each of your children, you will have many of these "trail markers" that remind you not just of your failures and mistakes but, more importantly, of the adjustments that enabled you to make progress.

In this journey of parenting, you will also have decisions to make as you come to forks in the trail. It's all about making the right choices that will lead you to a better place in the relationship. Not all decisions will be a choice between good and bad. Most times, it's choosing between something good and something better. The more you understand the dynamics of the relationship with your child, the more often you will make the better choice that leads to a maturing relationship where control is minimized and influence is maximized.

Parents Must Change

You might legitimately ask why the parents must change, or shift. It's because children grow and change in their needs and abilities whether we like it or not. They need different things from us at different levels of maturity. If we don't meet their needs, they will find someone who will. Wouldn't we rather they turn to us for information, insight, and advice? Who else is going to have their best interests at heart?

As children grow in their ability to question the reasons behind our rules, we need to improve our communication of those reasons. Likewise, as they develop the physical ability to assume household and family duties, we need to stop doing some things for them. And as they grow in their ability to draw their own conclusions to cultural information, we need to increase our listening and give them room to test their thoughts before we condemn or correct them.

In the next several chapters, we will focus on the changes you can, and should, make in response to the fact that you are naturally losing control of your children. Since controlling a child into adulthood is neither productive nor possible, you must think and act differently about the relationship with their children as they mature.

> CAUTION: Continued and determined attempts at parental control often have been the root cause of physical symptoms or emotional distress in teens and young adults, including chronic abdominal pain, eating disorders, cutting, addiction, and even suicide. It would be wrong to say that a controlling parent is the only cause of these disturbances, but it is often a major contributing factor. If you see any of these patterns emerging in your family, pay attention to the serious nature of these matters and get help to determine if control issues may be fueling the fire.

Parents must make changes to their ways of communicating with and responding to their children as they grow. Yes, change is scary, but I won't leave you to your own imagination as to what changes you need to make or how to implement them. In each of five upcoming chapters, we will explore how children typically change across a different age range and then discuss how we, as parents, can shift our thinking and our actions in response. Keep in mind, however, that every child is unique and matures at a different rate. Therefore, the age categories I've assigned to these chapters are generalizations.

Just know that you *must* shift.

Remember, it is the quality and characteristics of the relationship that will determine the future you have with your child. If you can transform your thinking and make the necessary shift, whatever the current age of your child, you can change resentment to respect, transform antagonism into admiration, and replace insolence with influence.

In the next chapter, we will look at some ways you can begin to connect meaningfully with your child that are not complicated or expensive yet can pave the way toward a mutually satisfying relationship.

CHAPTER 6

Does Your Child Feel the Love?

In talking with other parents about our own philosophy of raising children, it's easy to feel like we're pretty good parents. Sure, we know our record isn't spotless; we can readily admit that we've made small mistakes here and there in dealing with our kids. But we also know that many families who've encountered serious difficulty have done so because the parents made poor choices along the way. *We* plan—and hope—to avoid the same pitfalls. But do we really understand what it means to be a successful parent? And are we prepared to do what it takes to get there?

You might be surprised to learn that our success as parents hinges largely on what happens in a typical day and how we respond to it. John Maxwell, a leadership trainer and best-selling author, says the key to success in life is found in your daily agenda.[1] In other words, what you do day in and day out defines who you are and your level of success.

We are not measured by those rare days when we perform really well or do something special but, rather, by the many more average days when we're dealing with the ordinary demands of life. This is where the rubber meets the road, the times in life that are going to determine our success, whether it be in business, physical activity, financial management, or parenting. The activities we face repeatedly through most days and weeks are where we must focus our best efforts instead of trying to make up for lost time by planning a wonderful once-a-year vacation, a no-holds barred birthday bash, or a barrage of

Christmas gifts. Those are great to have in our lives, if possible, but they are not the fabric of life. And they will not be the things your children will look back on to determine whether they had a "good upbringing."

Knowing They're Loved Is Not Enough

One of my favorite authors on the parent–child relationship is Dr. Ross Campbell, who published his bestselling book *How to Really Love Your Child* in 1977. He brought many years' experience as a Christian child psychiatrist to bear on the practical and tangible advice he provided. The underlying idea is summed up in this quote: "Most parents love their children, but not all express their love in ways that the children *feel* loved."[2]

Feeling loved is not the same as being loved, but it is just as important. Research confirms that children who feel the affection of their parents are healthier physically and mentally, perform better academically, and have more positive relationships with friends and family. The converse is also true. Children who do not feel the affection of their parents have lower self-esteem and tend to be more hostile, aggressive, and antisocial.[2]

I firmly believe that love is *not* feelings; love is actions and thoughts. But the *feelings* of the one being loved are immensely important. When children do not feel loved, they do not behave or respond to others in a healthy way. The feeling of being valued or cherished changes everything. The day's agenda looks very different to us when we feel like a valued part of it. The instructions for every activity or assignment seem lighter when we feel the care of the instructor. When we feel someone has a genuine interest in us and knows our inner person, their rebuke or correction is much more likely to have a positive effect. On the other hand, when we doubt the love and concern our rebuker has for us, we usually respond with disrespect, disdain, or anger.

In his book *Relational Parenting*, Dr. Campbell tells the story of Mary, a young adult client who made a terrible mess of her life even though she was brought up in a stable, Christian home with parents who loved her. Before seeking help, Mary had dropped out of college, gotten pregnant, developed a drug addiction, and withdrawn from her family. "I love my parents and my family," she said, "and I had a good childhood. Nothing awful happened to me, as it did to so many of my friends. In fact, I don't really understand why I've made such a mess of things."

In his conversation with her parents, Dr. Campbell found they indeed deeply loved Mary but had somehow gotten the idea that they had to prevent her from becoming "spoiled." And so they resorted to correction and punishment as their primary way of relating to her. Dr. Campbell writes:

Mary revealed to me that she never felt that her parents deeply loved her. She knows in her mind that she was cared for while growing up, but she never has felt genuinely loved. Recognizing that feeling has been somewhat of a surprise to her, since she grew up in a nice home where her physical needs were generously provided for. In fact, she often feels confused and guilty for the poor relationship she has with her parents. Although she loves them, she has never been able to express this love. This inability makes her wonder if something is wrong with her. As a result, she tends to stay away from her parents, and is unable to communicate with them as she would like to.[4]

If we're to be effective parents, it's not enough for our children to *know* we love them. They need to *feel* our love. If they don't feel loved, they must work to convince themselves that we do love and care for them. So they struggle to know which inner voice to believe—the emotional voice that says, "My parents don't care about me," or the cognitive voice that says, "Of course they love me. They're my parents—they have to." The emotional voice has more power and is the more constant. Therefore, it has the greater effect on the child's actions and certainly his or her reactions.

Emotional needs are *real*, and they are *important*. Yet there are some simple steps you can take to increase the love your child feels coming from you. These steps involve changing the ways you express love so that it has meaning for your child and meets his or her emotional needs.

Filling Your Child's Emotional Fuel Tank

Imagine that your child, like a car or truck, has a tank inside where fuel is stored. Instead of gasoline, however, your child's tank holds positive feelings. When the tank is full, all is well. The child sees himself or herself as loved, accepted, valued, protected, understood, and encouraged. But as their tank gets depleted, children's feelings about themselves and the world around them become more negative, less hopeful. Some of your words and actions fill the tank, while other of your words and actions drain the tank.

We will focus here on the tank fillers, because that's where we usually need to change as parents. Following are three things you can do to fill your child's tank, and they correspond to the letters in the acronym EAT.

E = Eye Contact

E is for *eye contact*. You may have heard a someone call a son or daughter "the apple of my eye." This phrase is used to communicate a special relationship. Originally, the idiom actually referred to the pupil of the eye, and therein lies the first key to communicating love in a way that fills a child's emotional tank. Making direct eye contact with our children speaks volumes to them.

I experienced the power of eye contact with a mentor from my college years. My self-image was not severely poor, but I did feel inferior to my peers and not worthy of anyone's respect, especially those whom I greatly admired. Then a young businessman named Rodney began mentoring me and my friends. When he interacted with me in a social setting, Rodney would always look deeply into my eyes. In those brief moments, I felt like he knew me and truly valued me as an individual. This made me listen closely to every word he said and watch everything he did. I felt connected to him such that I was willing to share my goals, my fears, my thoughts, and my dreams with him. Rodney's simple act of making eye contact reassured me that he was safe and he really cared.

Making eye contact with your own children, regardless of their age, can have a similar impact on them. Just looking at their face is not good enough. Look into their pupils with interest and care. It is surprisingly uncomfortable at first, but it is so important and meaningful. Take every opportunity to gaze into their pupils with delight, especially while they're talking.

Children can tell when you are really looking at them. In fact, you can tell from a distance if someone is really looking at you. Have you had the experience of being in an audience when the speaker or singer made direct eye contact with you specifically? You know it when it happens. The effect is almost palpable, and it is powerful.

Eye contact is a tool so powerful that we must use it only for good with our children. Avoid using it in a negative way (or withholding it as a sign of disdain). Using eye contact as punishment is cruel, harmful, and dangerous. We've all felt someone's burning stare of disapproval and remember how uncomfortable it was. Do not take what was meant for good and turn it for evil.

I admit, making eye contact is difficult when we feel disappointment or disgust, and it's natural to want to avoid eye contact when we have been hurt. In those situations, we must be brave enough to calmly communicate how we feel, how we want to feel something different, and how we want the relationship to be better for everyone involved. So if tension is high between you and your child and it's not resolving, eye contact can still be part of building a bridge across the gulf the separates you. The older the child, the greater the divide can be, but seeking to refuel your son's or daughter's emotional tank through eye contact is well worth the effort.

Practicing eye contact is sometimes helpful. To do so, find a friend who has a two- to three-month-old baby. Stare into the baby's pupils for thirty seconds and feel how he or she is soaking it up. If the baby withdraws, maybe you're not conveying a warm, or "soft," look and need to release some tension in your face. The baby will respond to the message you are sending through your eyes. Babies are like mirrors in that they usually reflect back the message they're receiving. And in many ways, your children will do the same.

A = Attention

The *A* in EAT stands for *attention*. Specifically, it means *focused* attention.

We've all seen a child tugging at his mother's clothes and crying, "Mama, Mama, Mama," while the mother is cooking or in a conversation. If the mother ignores the child, the cycle repeats itself again and again until, finally, the mother turns and shouts, "What do you want?!?" This is often a frustrated response, not meant to discover the child's need but, rather, to get him to be quiet. It's especially infuriating to the mom when the child no longer remembers what he wanted to tell her in the first place.

Often the child's need in such situations is not to talk but to be noticed, to get the parent's attention. Their emotional tank is crying out, "Give me some fuel!" It can save a lot of time and aggravation—as well as meet the child's need—if we will stop, bend down to his eye level, and give him focused attention for five seconds. To a child, five seconds is a long time and communicates meaning.

Focused attention is a way that sends the message "You are important to me." Children feel loved when their parents listen to what they are saying and watch what they are doing. Simply saying the words as you continue doing something else is not the same. Really listen to the meaning behind the child's words, or the emotions within the words, and respond to that with sincerity. Maybe the appropriate response is "Wow! That's amazing!" or "I'm so sorry, Honey." Or maybe it's a warm hug.

Next time you're at a playground, listen to how children appeal for their parent's attention. The child at the top of the slide cries out, "Daddy, Daddy! Watch me!" Or the kid on the swing repeatedly looks to see if Mom is watching. Children want the cheers of their parents, but more importantly, they long for the focused attention.

Bedtime is a critical time, especially for young children. It is the perfect time for a parent to give focused attention, even if there's more than one child in the room. Instead of hustling them off to bed with threats or counting, spend some time in their bedroom listening to their silliness, telling them stories, or singing a song. This is focused attention, and it refuels their emotional tanks.

Teens typically burst into your bedroom as you are getting ready for bed or even dropping off to sleep, and that's when they want to tell you all about their feelings regarding a friend or event. They seem get these sudden urges to talk at the most inconvenient times. But if you're not willing to give them your attention when they ask for it, they will stop talking to you. That's why you need to commit now to giving your child your focused attention whenever it's requested.

Give your children as much time as you can afford. The example of Susanna Wesley has given much encouragement to mothers of multiple children. The mother of future Methodist ministers John Wesley and Charles Wesley, Susanna had ten children yet managed to schedule an hour with each child in the evening, rotating through the kids on different days of the week. She made a plan that worked for her home. It will look differently in yours, but a plan to give focused attention will go a long way toward communicating love to your children. Some time is better than no time.

Be pleasant, be relaxed, and be present.

Your children want and need your attention.

T = Touch

The final letter in EAT stands for *touch*. Boys and girls of all ages need the physical touch of a parent. If the only time they experience your touch is when you are angry or frustrated, it's a double negative. Your touch must provide comfort and reassurance of your child's value to you. How many times have you touched your child's skin with your own today? How about this week?

I don't pretend to understand the wonder of skin-to-skin contact, but there is something about human touch that causes our emotional beings to respond. Let me be clear that I am not talking about erotic sexual touch with children; that is clearly out of bounds. That is the kind of touch that violates a child's trust and has resulted in much harm to many. But holding your child's hand when crossing the street, touching your daughter's face, running your fingers through your son's hair—these moments send strong messages of care and concern.

When my oldest children were in high school, we were intently studying communication together as a family and found some very interesting material on the power of touch. Studies have been conducted to determine what kinds of touch most strongly communicate value. One such study compared three types of touch: face-to-face, hand-to-hand, and hand-to-head. We were surprised at the results.

The touch of lowest power and significance was face-to-face. My passionate teenagers could not believe that kissing ranked so low! Movies and romance novels focus much on the power of the kiss, yet real measurement of the impact revealed that face-to-face contact ranked pretty low in long-term impact for communicating the sincere value of another.

Next in power was hand-to-hand touch. How many times has a child walked more confidently in the dark when holding Daddy's hand, feeling safe? How many times have children walked proudly into a room of peers while holding the hand of a parent? Even adults experience feelings of security and warmth when holding hands with another. Hand-to-hand touch definitely communicates concern, care, and protection. Don't be surprised when your child needs the comfort and security of feeling your hand in theirs. Also keep in mind the power of holding the hand of a grandmother, a sick friend who is in the hospital, or a child who is lost.

The most powerful of the three kinds of touch the study examined was hand-to-head. If you stop to think about it, we know this intuitively. When we look endearingly into the face of a person we adore, we instinctively want to reach out to stroke their hair or hold their face in our hands. These are not casual touches. Hand-to-head touches clearly communicate a deep level of care, high value, and genuine interest.

Rubbing the curly top of your five-year-old son means more to him than we can imagine. Wiping tears from your daughter's face gently adds fuel to her emotional tank as does a caring hand laid on the back of her neck as you walk along.

In the Smith household, we did a lot of touching. In the early years, it looked like a bunch of monkeys climbing up a tree as my kids would hang all over me or vie for a piggyback ride. Then there were the wrestling matches in the living room, where we tried to not break the furniture or lamps. Later, it was high fives, hugs, chest bumps, handshakes, and pats on the back.

Fuel your children's emotional tank by remembering EAT:

E = Eye Contact
A = Attention
T = Touch

A Word of Caution

These tools are not to be used to manipulate your children, or as "techniques" for making your child better. The idea is not to make your children (or anyone else) think you care more than you do. Rather, I'm trying to help you more effectively express the sincere level of care and concern you already possess. Children seem to come equipped with a highly sensitive "fake meter." Faking it might work on some adults, but it won't cut it with children.

Use these tools to communicate real love and sincere interest, but do so with your heart set on giving, not getting. Be determined to fill your children's emotional tanks so they can soar in life. Maybe you didn't have someone do this for you, but you can certainly do it for them.

Time to Take Inventory

Pause for a minute and take an inventory of the relationships you have with friends and neighbors. What feelings do you experience when you see a particular name appear on your caller ID? Some names may cause dread while others make you feel a tinge of excitement. Why is that?

Even if you agree that we all need to feel loved, evaluating your current adult relationships can be a great exercise. By evaluating the good and bad relationships in your life, you can gain useful insights into how you need to improve your communication with others. To make progress in this area, you must be prepared to change.

The most important relationships in your life are the ones inside your own home, and they deserve your greatest attention. Indeed, these relationships have the potential for the greatest return.

Remember that no one else can be the mother or father you were designed to be, and your child doesn't want anyone else, regardless of anything they may have said to you. In the end, children want *their* parents to love them, to care for them, to be proud of them. *You* are the apple of *their* eye!

This brings us to the first aspect of communicating love.

CHAPTER 7

Reeling in the Early Years: Building a Foundation for Freedom

The title of Robert Fulghum's mega-bestseller *All I Really Need to Know I Learned in Kindergarten* underscores the importance of a person's early years. While humorous, this phrase holds a lot of truth. Within the context of parenting, managing well during a child's early childhood certainly sets the stage for success in navigating the parent-child relationship as time goes on.

Because the application of the relationship principles we're discussing looks different across the various stages of a child's physical and emotional development, each of the next few chapters will focus on a different developmental stage. HOWEVER, I urge you not to skip ahead in the book to the stage you're currently dealing with, because kids at earlier stages have specific needs you may have overlooked. You will find it helpful to understand and address any unmet needs with age-appropriate responses as you seek to deepen the relationship with your child and build influence. This is especially true if the child is a foster or adopted child who came to your home at a later stage of development.

Establishing Control Early

Earlier, I said that influence is the key to completing the parenting journey successfully. Does this mean parenting is all about influence? Not at all! Establishing control during the early childhood stage is essential. Yes, parents must shift their emphasis toward influence as the child matures, but trying to influence a toddler with logic and explanation is futile and an incorrect application of the concept.

As infants, of course, children need us to control everything since they're unable to decide much of anything. What infant prefers a particular brand of diaper? Or chooses whether to take immunizations? We, as the parents, must exercise control as a starting point, and it is through control that we initially teach our children boundaries. Rules and regulations are very important for the toddler. Clear boundaries communicate what is okay and safe for the child and actually create an atmosphere of freedom within the confines of what is known to be approved.

During the early years, when the focus is on rules and regulations, parents must communicate to the child which rules are flexible and which are unbending. For example, if your family has a rule that the child must drink from a cup or wear a shirt at the family meal, you can be flexible in allowing the child to choose the color of her cup or shirt. When there is no choice—if the favorite cup is being used by a sibling or the desired shirt is dirty—this should be clearly and kindly communicated. If the child feels disappointed, use the situation to train her to understand that all is not lost when her choices are limited.

A word of caution, however. My deceased father-in-law gave me some great advice when one of my toddlers was "throwing a fit" over a minor issue. He said, "His problem doesn't seem like much to you, but to him, it's the biggest problem he has. So have a little compassion." Compassion can go a long way to helping your little ones accept a sense of loss. Sometimes their unwillingness to move past the problem may need a little nudge, but it's important to feel their pain and sense of losing control over one of the few choices available to them.

Concerning this issue of a child's crying or pouting at not being able to make a choice he usually gets to make, like the desired cup is in the dishwasher or has been chosen by someone else, you can help prepare him for the disappointment. If you know his choice is unavailable, help him to anticipate it by saying something like, "Let me see if I can find the blue cup. I think someone has already used it. I see other colors, but I'm not finding a blue one. What would be your next choice?" Giving children the sensation of being disappointed before the actual pronouncement that they're not getting their choice helps them try to control their emotional response. In no way am I suggesting this will prevent all temper tantrums, but it's a small step toward training children to manage the emotions that happen when confronted with disappointment in life. And your compassion toward your children in these situations helps to soothe their hurt.

On the other hand, when a rule is unbending and non-negotiable, children should have a clear sense of that fact. For instance, buckling into a car seat is a firm rule that should be non-negotiable and therefore met with automatic obedience. In such cases, it is not about a parent's control over the child but, rather, about the fact we all are subject to certain rules that are non-negotiable. For this reason, we must develop a cheerful acceptance of those constraints. As parents, it is our job to model cheerfulness as much as possible and talk about the things "we must do" before we try forcing children to do them.

A Child Is Not a Lab Rat

In the early childhood years, the parts of the brain that process logic and manage emotions are not fully developed. Knowing this should affect how we should train our children, recognizing they are not ready to understand the reasons behind our rules or the implications of disobeying them. When we refer to "the faith of a little child," we're really talking about trust. The fact is, children depend on trust because their ability to grasp abstract ideas is greatly limited, as is their ability to reach conclusions using logic.

Punishment for violating clearly communicated boundaries helps children to form a clear association between crossing boundaries and the resulting harm. The right method of punishment is widely debated, but the heart of the punishment is what I want to address here. Any punishment that causes injury requiring healing—be it physical, psychological, or emotional—is going beyond correction. The heart of any punishment should be corrective and restorative. The desire of the parent should be to use the least amount of punishment necessary to achieve a correction in the desires, or heart, of the child.

The goal is not *correct behavior*; the goal is *correct desires*. If the child's desires are right, good behavior will follow. Focusing all our attention on the child's behavior is the path of control, and it leads to a destination neither you nor your child will like.

This approach to child training is known as behavior modification. The theory of behavior modification came from research with lab rats in the 1950s and has never been shown to be appropriate or effective in humans. The concepts of positive reinforcement (giving a reward for desired behavior) and negative reinforcement (removing something desirable for undesirable behavior) began being applied to parenting in the 1960s and 1970s without considering the long-term effects on emotionally complex human beings. This focus on controlling or modifying behavior in the absence of concern for the emotional needs of the child has contributed to many serious problems in our culture as evidenced by rampant self-centeredness, marked disrespect, loss of moral boundaries, and weakened character.

If behavior modification worked with humans, it would make parenting much easier. We could simply set the parameters to reward desired behaviors, remove rewards for undesirable behaviors, and all our problems would be solved. Because it sounds so simple, this approach attracts many. But it doesn't work, and you should flee from anyone who is teaching this type of manipulation!

Be on the alert for parenting programs or books that promise solutions with "Five Easy Steps" or "Three Simple Ways." The language alone should tell you their teachings are not rooted in a relationship but, rather, in manipulation. Do you like being manipulated? Neither do your children, so steer clear.

Proactive vs. Reactive Parenting

Many parenting authors and teachers who focus on punishment as the foundation of their approach to child training often cite the many scriptural passages about discipline. These Bible passages are reliably true, but in many cases their meaning is misinterpreted or misapplied. Discipline is training. The biblical concept of discipline is best understood in the relationship between a teacher and a disciple, or follower. This relationship is one of closeness, instruction, training, and imitation.

Though discipline may involve punishment, it's a very small part of it. Discipline should be 90 percent teaching and practice and only 10 percent punishment. If punishment takes a more prominent role in your home, you need to reconsider your approach.

The teaching of the Bible in regard to discipline—as in the traditions of many cultures—is rooted in building relationships, not in correcting behavior. This approach is sometimes referred to as *proactive* parenting versus *reactive* parenting. Proactive parenting focuses on the needs of the child, both present and future. Proactive parents will guide their child into right thinking and right actions, whereas reactive parents focus on a current undesirable behavior and seek to stop it.

Reactive parenting is akin to a doctor treating the patient's symptoms rather than curing the disease. The outward activity of undesirable behavior is merely a symptom of what's going on in the child's heart. Looking beneath the surface to determine the child's inner needs is more complicated and difficult than simply treating the symptoms, but addressing the root cause will have better, longer-lasting effects.

Placing heavy emphasis on punishment as the primary means of discipline is, by definition, reactive parenting. When the child strays out of bounds, a painful or angry response from the parent follows. The reactive parent often uses a loud voice, threats, or physical aggression to produce fear of disobedience. Waiting until a child is out of bounds before making adjustments to his actions or attitudes is much like waiting to turn the steering wheel of a car until the tires are already off the road—there will be much trauma to all involved.

When my youngest sons were nine and ten years old, they wanted to raise pigs for the 4-H livestock show. Jan and I knew absolutely nothing about pigs beyond the taste of bacon, but we jumped in "whole hog" to raise a couple of show pigs. We soon learned that cute little piglets grow into big old hogs. Thankfully, we got some good advice on handling the animals.

We were advised that in addition to the usual feeding and watering, the pigs needed to be walked every day for exercise. So our sons took those two little pigs down a one-mile trail each day, using a three-foot-long tree limb to guide them and encourage them to keep moving. The boys learned that lightly touching the pigs on their side would cause them to move away from the stick and back onto the path. Not until they grew into 300-pound hogs did it become clear to us how important these walks actually were. The pigs had been learning daily that they couldn't just do whatever entered their minds to do. By gently guiding them while they were young, the boys trained them to be guided later in life when, frankly, the pigs had the physical power to do whatever they wanted.

We thought the daily exercise had been prescribed to develop the pigs' muscles, and it did at that. But more importantly, the exercise was training both the owners and animals to give and receive instruction while learning to trust and cooperate. At the livestock show, each hog was taken to a show ring where it was guided across an open space for the judges to examine. The hog was not afraid of the rod but was willing to trust the instruction from the familiar boy, even in an unfamiliar environment. Jan and I watched our sons and their charges in amazement as if seeing a beautiful relationship unfold.

Raising show pigs seemed so easy that first year, we then decided to raise *eight* pigs the following year. About this time, someone else told us the pigs didn't really need all that walking. "They'll grow just fine if you give them unlimited feed and water," we were told. "Save yourself all that trouble." And so we did. Day after day, those pigs ate and drank untended in their pen. And boy, did they grow! Even without exercise, these eight pigs grew to be as big as the previous two.

The trouble came when it was time to go to the show. These eight 300-pound hogs decided they did not want to get into the trailer. They had never taken instruction from us before, and they weren't about to start now! I thought I would outsmart them and trick them into the trailer, but it turns out hogs are smarter than they look. So I tried physically pulling them or pushing them, but hogs are stronger that they look, too. I soon found myself unexpectedly riding a hog that was determined to take me out! Not only was I tired and frustrated, but I also got hurt in the process. And then anger set in.

Do you see any parallels to parenting?

This is a picture of the path reactive parenting will take you and your family. But the point at which you experience fatigue, frustration, pain, and anger is not the end of the path. Hopelessness is.

Families that never move away from reactive parenting establish a pattern of pain and discomfort that makes them avoid one another. The result is that teen and adult children become estranged from their parents rather than seeking refuge and comfort in their family. It's a sad state of affairs, especially in families made up of "good people" who only want to "do what is right," who want to love and be loved.

The Path to Proactive Parenting

Becoming a proactive parent is essential to creating or restoring a warm, loving, cooperative family environment. This mindset will lead to daily practices within the family that in many ways resemble the daily "hog walks" my sons took with their animals. There is something magical about a calm, consistent, kind guidance that children (and hogs) respond to when it begins early and continues long enough to develop trust.

To be a proactive parent, you must first decide where you want to go as a family and what you want to become. Deciding the core values of your family—the most important character traits you want to develop in your children—will guide your decisions and actions better than a set of rules and regulations. The rules and regulations should be visible evidence of your goals but are not the goals themselves or the measure of your parenting success.

Of course, during the toddler years, rules may not be related to character as much as they are related to safety. No doubt, obedience and trust are character traits, so rules that are aimed at maintaining safety still contribute to character development.

Consider a few examples. Training a toddler to immediately obey a command "stop!" is not simply obedience training, it is safety training. Toddlers notoriously put themselves in danger, such as approaching a street, picking up a knife, reaching out to an animal, or touching pots on the stove. The more imminent the danger, the clearer the need for prior training. If a child has not been trained to respond to your voice, you lose the ability to protect them when they are out of your reach.

Training young children to pick up toys thoroughly is not only for your sanity, but begins the foundation of building the character trait of diligence that will be required later for putting away important documents or expensive and necessary tools. Similarly, training an attitude of responsibility may begin with a youngster memorizing and repeating the phrase, "What can I do to help?" Our response to the question with a simple task like removing a plate from the table or putting a shoe in its place can reinforce the importance of the memorized question.

Even the training of kindness to a sibling is not simply to create a peaceful home, but it is foundational training for a life of being kind to others. The earlier the training of kindness begins, the more it becomes part of the fabric of their personal values and character.

It is the parent's responsibility to take the training seriously. In the toddler and pre-school years, any attitudes or acts of disobedience that may pose a threat to parental authority must be addressed early and consistently. The goal is to give correction in a way that promotes not only desired behavior, but also the character and mindset behind it that will carry them into a life of right living.

Correction of behavior that is "out of bounds" is one important part of discipline and requires clear communication. Before a child comprehends the language you speak, one of the few means of correction he or she will understand is pain. The pain is simply a language, a communication tool, and should not be meant as repayment. Let me underscore that I mean the *least amount of pain needed* to accomplish a change of desire. No injury, no harm. Just enough to deter. And it should never be applied in anger. Remember, the pain is simply a language, and should not be meant as repayment. As in the case of the hog walks, early correction applied firmly but gently works best.

As children's understanding of language develops, the issue becomes whether they understand or believe the parent's instruction. The reason for correction begins to shift from *what* they are doing to *why* they are doing it. If children clearly know the boundaries set for them, then they are straying out of bounds because they don't believe you mean it or because they think the rule is not as important as their desire. Correction during this period is very important because it is beginning to address inner qualities like trust, submission, self-restraint, and delayed gratification—important qualities they will need in order to handle freedom.

Several years ago, a friend told me of an experience he had with his daughter. She was about eight months old at the time and was at the stage of scooting or crawling. In their home was a gas space-heater with a bright-red knob for adjusting the flame. The first time the little girl reached for the brightly colored knob, her father sternly told her, "No! Don't touch!" and moved her away from the heater. He may have swatted her hand, though I don't recall specifically.

What I do remember was his uncertainty whether she understood what he had tried to communicate. After placing her back on the floor, he watched her behavior closely. At first, she seemed to be uninterested in his presence as she played with her toys. After several minutes, she again noticed the red knob and began moving toward it. When she finally got within arm's length, she began reaching out to touch the knob but then stopped and looked over her shoulder to see if her father was watching.

The question about his daughter's understanding was answered without a word. She clearly knew she was to not touch the knob but didn't know whether she would get caught or corrected. In this case, the father was engaged, observant, and responsive. Some eight years after the incident, the relationships in that home testify to the loving, gentle, but firm guidance that characterized the discipline of the parents.

Parents Are Trainers

When Jan and I first started working with horses, we knew the head from the tail and not much more. We both had some experience riding as children, though I remember as a boy spending about as much time in the dirt as I did in the saddle.

In training our horses, we have found that the approach called "natural horsemanship" makes the most sense and produces the most reliable results. The idea is to seek to lay hold of the horse's willingness to cooperate, as opposed to the traditional idea of "breaking" a horse's will to bring it under submission.

The natural horsemanship approach begins with a confrontational period that is not oppressive or harmful but clearly establishes two facts: 1) The human is in charge, and 2) the human is safe. When the horse begins to show that it wants to resolve the conflict, the trainer relaxes the confrontation and allows the horse to cooperate and listen for further instruction. With every new command, more attention is given until the instruction is understood. Freedom is the test that reveals whether the horse will continue to follow the command or "needs more schooling."

When punishment is used, it is only enough to get the horse's attention and reinforce that the command was real and the horse should listen to the trainer, not its own thoughts or feelings. The focus is on building a willing, trusting relationship in which the horse desires to please the trainer and becomes responsive to the smallest request, not out of fear but out of desire. This is what horsemen call "join up," meaning horse and rider are no longer opponents but teammates.

Children are not horses, but the relationship between a natural horseman and his animal is reflective of a healthy parent–child relationship that is intentionally guided toward mutual respect and mutual benefit. All the work is meant to achieve freedom for the child, not indefinite control by the parent. However, the pursuit of freedom begins with establishing control so that trust can develop. Trust is the confidence the trainee has that the trainer values him completely and will not intentionally seek to harm him, whether the trainee be a horse or child.

Parents are the trainers in the home. It is our job to pursue relationships within the family that allow for freedom. However, freedom cannot be the starting point; freedom has no meaning unless children know their boundaries and understand the behavior expected of them. A boundary may be the limit of what is safe, such as not touching a hot stove or not standing near a ledge. But a boundary may also be value-based, such as not coloring on the wall or unrolling the toilet paper. In either case, a baby or toddler is not able to use logic to understand the boundary or rule. However, he will associate a consequence with the act of going out of bounds. The consistency of the consequences trains the child to trust and obey the parent.

As the trainer of a young child, you must begin by establishing the boundaries and control that lead to trust. Remember, trust means the child has confidence that you completely value them, that you would not intentionally harm them, and that you desire good for them. The kind of trust that enables a child to believe his parent is acting in his best interest should not be taken lightly. Indeed, it is our duty as parents to exemplify the kind of character worthy of trust. Any act of punishment a parent renders must carry with it the weight of responsibility to be careful not to harm but to adequately correct the child and restore him to a close relationship with the parent.

Any pain involved in a child's training must communicate that the parent believes the child is able to follow the instructions that have been given for her good. Consider a specific example of using pain as a language and a training tool: A nursing four-month-old begins to use her new teeth to bite between sucks. The biting must stop. If removing the child from the breast does not clearly communicate to her that biting is not allowed, and if words or cries of pain do not have the desired effect, the mother must begin to time a pinch (or other source of pain) at the onset of biting along with the word the family will use for "stop." The pinch is not retaliation; it's training. The intention is not to harm the child or to release the mother's anger; it's to stop a wrong action. Sounds like reactive parenting, doesn't it? It would be if the pinch were focused merely on stopping the bite. Yes, the initial goal is to train the child to respond to the family's word for "stop," but ultimately (perhaps several years in the future) it will help the child to understand a reason for obedience. This will require consistency.

Pain at this age is not punishment as much as it is training. Consider a baby on a changing table with a dirty diaper. Is there a reason for the child to lie still until the deed is done, or is it just a control issue for the parent? The child senses no danger, no reason to refrain from wiggling and rolling, yet the parent knows there's danger in falling four feet to the floor. Having never experienced the fall, the child does not understand. But he can understand that every time he tries to turn over on the table there's a sharp sting on his leg and a word for "stop." He also should begin to associate lying on his back during the procedure with hearing a pleasant voice and receiving some emotionally satisfying eye contact.

The pain used in training may not always be physical pain, but it should never be the pain of rejection, as can happen when we angrily send a child from our presence. Sending a child away delivers a very confusing message. Most children interpret it to mean that we don't want them, we don't like them, or we wish they weren't there. Of course we want a close relationship with our children, but in the heat of the moment, our emotions often cause us to do or say things that send a very different message. This is especially true when we wait too long to address a situation. Then our emotions get involved, and we start sending the wrong signals.

One day, I was home when a son of eight or nine years old was really frustrating my wife. The tension had risen to near the boiling point, and still the boy was continuing his defiance. I don't actually remember the issue behind the conflict, but I do remember that it was a pivotal moment in our relationship with that son. I decided to step in when I was certain the next words from my wife's mouth were going to be "Get out of my sight! Go to your room!" The situation had not yet sucked me into an emotional response, and I was still able to see the boy's pain and frustration that was veiled from my wife by her own feelings. In that moment, Jan trusted me enough to help her calm down and approach the issue another way.

I knew she wanted more than obedience from our son. She wanted closeness, and she wanted to nurture a right spirit within him. Separation was going to accomplish neither of those goals. Jan and I talked about it, and we committed to draw our son physically close to us every time he showed anger, frustration, or resistance to sound instruction. And indeed, we discovered he needed *more* affirmation, *more* affection, and *more* physical touch. He needed fewer words of correction. His emotional tank was running low, and he was crying out with the only expression he could manage—resistance. We are forever thankful for that day when we began choosing to pull him close with touches and hugs instead of pushing him away.

Training Opportunities with Small Children

Teaching and training a child from birth to five years does not have to involve pain. In fact, pain as a tool of discipline should disappear as soon as understanding and desire to obey appears. Consider the example of training a child to not touch a hot stove. Allowing the child to touch a hot stove could itself cause pain in the training, but it would also cause injury, which we have already established is bad. Because we teach children not to touch hot things for his safety, a slap on a child's outreached hand is far better than allowing him to touch the stove. But could the training be accomplished with no pain at all?

Keep in mind this training is all about helping a child make a connection in his developing brain between heat and harm. Start with a stove or pot only warm enough that you don't want to leave your hand on it. While using words for "hot," allow the child to get close enough to feel the heat, thus helping him to associate the words and your concern with the sensation of heat. The words and tone must tell him he is near something harmful.

Training children about boundaries can begin in infancy, such as teaching a baby to stay on a blanket and play with her toys within a defined space. The blanket provides her with a clear, visible boundary. At first, you can use physical barriers and words to indicate that the edge of the blanket is the boundary, and then add a small sting when the child attempts to move off the blanket. Again, no injury, no harm—just helping her to recognize the safety and freedom within the boundary and to connect crossing the boundary with consequences. At first, you should have low expectations for the infant's understanding and response, but over days or weeks, progress will be made. If not, don't get entrenched on this issue. It's just an example, not a milestone or rite of passage.

Another important training opportunity is to teach a child to sit on your lap quietly until given permission to get down to play. In much the same way killer whales are taught to jump over a rope, you must start with very low expectations and focus on the child's achieving success. A whale's trainers start by laying the rope on the bottom of the pool. Every time the whale swims over it, they give it a fish. The rope is gradually moved higher and higher, and each time the whale crosses the rope, it receives a reward. Finally, when the rope is lifted out of the water, the whale still easily clears the rope in expectation of its reward, and the whale has learned to jump!

In a similar way, practice with a small child by sitting her on your lap for thirty seconds and helping her watch the second hand on a watch or clock. Repeat this exercise several times over a week. Then tell her you want her to show you she can sit quietly and still for a full minute. Celebrate her success with praise, touch, and eye contact. Continue to increase the time as you feel comfortable.

But the real training comes when you tell her, "You've done so well and are getting so big that I want you to sit with me for a while, and I'm not going to tell you how long. But I know you can do it. If you can't be still, then you can ask to get down. But you can't get down until I give you permission." This is when you begin to build trust and cooperation.

The ability to sit quietly is important in many situations like traveling, attending public functions, and visiting a doctor's office. The child's success with this facet of training opens a world of opportunities for the whole family, and reduces a common point of contention between parents and small children.

Practicing the act of having a child come to you immediately when his name is called is also good for everyone. Additionally, it is a very real safety measure; waiting to train a child until he's already in danger doesn't work. Start when he is a few feet away, and explain that it's a game in which he will be rewarded with a kiss, a hug, or occasionally a treat. Sometimes it should be just an "attaboy" so he doesn't learn to associate obedience with receiving something. Then it will be your responsibility to use the child's name carefully to call him, not to threaten him with it. He will associate his name with a need to respond now—a good habit that will also help you to protect him from unforeseen dangers.

When Parents Fail to Establish Control

Again, establishing parental control during the early childhood years is essential. Yet as a practicing physician, I see many cases where parents have not been able or willing to establish control, resulting in a variety of health issues. One that immediately comes to mind is dental care. With very few exceptions, unhealthy teeth in children is the result of poor attention on the part of their parents. Don't be duped into thinking you are the exception if your child's teeth are rotten or filled with cavities. Most dental problems are preventable. But without control, parents cannot effectively care for their children's teeth.

Many parents tell me, "But she won't let me brush her teeth!" as if this is an adequate excuse. But the truth is, it's simply an admission of guilt on the part of the parent to teach and train the child. It takes time to train children in the habits of personal hygiene, and it is usually inconvenient. But every minute spent on this training prevents the time and expense of dental work and saves the child from a good deal of future pain and discomfort.

Begin early with a washcloth, wiping the emerging teeth of a baby before progressing to a toothbrush. Brushing must become an expected part of the routine of life where control is first established by the parent, then later released to the child as a life habit. This is a good illustration of the adage, "Sow a thought, reap an action; sow an action, reap a habit; sow a habit, reap a lifestyle."

A similar situation I commonly encounter is a child's failure to respond to the prescribed treatment of a simple condition. Follow-up questions often reveal that the medicine was actually never given because "She wouldn't take it" or "He would clench his mouth" or

"She spits it out." I understand that children often don't want to take their medicine, but they also don't want to go to bed, take a bath, eat certain foods, put on shoes, or a host of other things that are good for them. This is just further evidence that some parents are unwilling to endure the struggle of gaining control as a basis of training for the good of the child.

These parents need to understand that their children will eventually submit to persistent efforts and communication that is direct, calm, and respectful of their children's fears. Keep in mind, these battles for control are helping the child progress toward a life of freedom and self-control. Without a learned willingness to submit to a loving authority, they will not be able to submit to self-control. And self-control is the goal.

As parents, we must be the kind of influence in the lives of our children that causes them to grow into bigger and better people just because they have been with us. The proverb states, "Iron sharpens iron, and one man sharpens another."[1] The sharpening process involves friction and sometimes sparks, but it is always working toward a good result. What may not be immediately evident in this proverb is that as one sharpens the other, the first one is also sharpened, or improved. This should be true of parenting as well. Remember, the training process won't always be comfortable, but when done faithfully and correctly, it is continually moving both parent and child toward mutual benefit.

Words Matter

One final thought for this age group involves the words we speak. At first, babies and toddlers not only must learn our words and language but also how to say the words and the meaning of them. Parents get so excited when children begin to associate the right word with the right item, whether it be the dog, a ball, or Mama. Our little ones then begin to string words together into sentences and attempt conversations, and we start thinking they understand us.

But developmentally, children continue in a phase called "concrete association," or concrete reasoning, for several years. This limits their ability to interpret the instructions we give them, as well the reasoning behind our guidance. Although it seems obvious to us that the child should avoid touching a hot stove, take his medicine regardless of taste or texture, and should only cross the street with an adult, the ability to see the value behind the words requires logic or abstract thought—processes that are typically not developed until later stages.

Five-year-old children love stories, and they love jokes even more. Our oldest son was five when he came home one afternoon from visiting his friend next door. He had learned a joke and was so excited to tell it to us! Here is how he told it: "Why did the little monster throw the butter out the window? Because he wanted to SEE IT FLY! Hahahahaha!" Although he understood the language and all the words, he couldn't grasp the abstract nature of the joke and therefore could not make the transition in his mind from *butter* to *butterfly*. He was still in the concrete association phase, so in his mind he saw only butter flying out the window. All he knew was that the joke was in some way funny, and so he laughed and expected us to do the same.

A few years later, I was reading nursery rhymes to my children and came across the story of Jack and Jill. After reading the part where "Jack fell down and broke his crown," I asked the children what they thought it meant that Jack " broke his crown." My five-year-old daughter looked at me as if I had asked a silly question. "You know, Daddy! Ugh! It's what you color with!" I was so surprised! She thought I had said "crayon" because it's what made sense to her concrete thinking in listening to the story. After all, Daddy the Doctor should know that it's easier to break a crayon than to crack a cranium!

So often, parents give instructions that children cannot accept because they require abstract thinking to interpret the words. Take, for example, "You must share." Sharing is a complex concept barely understood by many adults and certainly not by two-year-old children. To them, sharing looks like "The other child gets it, and I don't." A better substitute is "take turns" or some similar phase to indicate that ownership or use of a thing is time-limited. Training with this concept can be done with Play-Doh and a single cookie cutter, having one child pass the cutter to the other child and back in a short time lasting a few seconds. Gradually lengthening the time of waiting trains children to have the expectation "my turn" is coming. This type of exercise provides children a concrete experience for an abstract idea.

Keep in mind that no amount of punishment will help a child cross over from concrete to abstract reasoning, but taking a heavy hand with punishment may well delay the journey. Discipline in the early years should mostly be positive and pleasant and promote the feeling that you and your child are on the same team, that you are seeking to help him understand the world around him, and it is better for him to control himself. As his self-control increases, your child is becoming ready for increased freedom and responsibility.

CHAPTER 8

Finding Their Way: Teaching Responsibility in the Elementary Years

Children between the ages of six and nine—we'll call these the elementary years—*need* responsibility. Skills, understanding, and willpower come together to make school-aged children able to do many things, and you'll find they *want* to be responsible. During their early years, concrete thinking limited much of their ability. But in the elementary years, they transition to abstract thinking. This change allows for leaps forward in ability, resulting in a real eagerness to do things. As parents, we must adjust our communication and expectations to capitalize on the child's eagerness in this stage.

The parental shift from control to influence usually happens over a number of years, but it must have a beginning and must be intentional. It is in these elementary years that much of the transition should happen regarding how we relate to our children. Influence, which will become critical in the teen years, is forged in a relationship of mutual respect and trust—a relationship where both parent and child like each other and each feels valued by the other. Trust can be easily built during the elementary years, so it's important for parents to take advantage of this time and implement responsibility training.

If parents fail to trust children in this stage with responsibility and train them to manage it, a great opportunity is lost. These children may still grow to be healthy adults, but this missed opportunity is a setback they will have to expend great effort to overcome. Likewise, their parents will face greater struggles to build trust and influence down the road.

The Urge to Achieve

Training is very important at every stage, as we build on the previous stage and lay the foundation for the next. Just as a baseball pitcher must learn proper body position and throwing mechanics through many hours of training and repetition before taking the mound in the big leagues, the training and practice of responsibility prepares children for what awaits them in life. Therefore, we must resist training our children to be irresponsible in this stage, because it will be much harder for them to reverse bad habits later.

How do we train our children to be irresponsible? By not trusting them with real responsibility. No responsibility is irresponsibility. One of the favorite sayings in our house is, "If you want children to be responsible, give them responsibility." When parents hear this, they often think of trying to get a teenager off the couch, phone, or computer in order to do chores. But the time to apply this approach is during the elementary years when developing abilities in language, understanding, abstract reasoning, and physical coordination are coming together in an exciting way for kids. This is when motivation to put their newly discovered abilities to use is at an all-time high. They may say they want to do a task for you, but in reality, they want to do the task for themselves.

New challenges and accomplishments are exciting for elementary-aged kids. Watching children of this age play reveals they have transitioned from the fun of knocking down a tower of building blocks to the excitement of building a tower. I refer to this transition as moving from destruction to construction. And they get serious about adding to the list of constructive things they are able to do such as ride a bike, throw a ball, climb a tree, read words on a page, use a knife, carry in groceries, operate light machinery, and so on. They become nonstop whirlwinds of construction, and it is imperative that their parents recognize this and fan the flames of this growing desire to achieve.

Discovering Your Child's Natural Bent

Every child's drive is different, but each will have a desire to grow in competence in some way. One child may appear more outwardly competitive while another may quietly go about gaining new skills, but the desire to grow is naturally present in all kids at this age. Each of my four children behaved differently when it came to this stage, and we didn't always recognize the future significance of what they were doing, but all were busy taking their first steps onto a personal path.

You're probably familiar with the Bible's admonition "Train up a child in the way he should go, and when he is old, he will not depart from it."[1] The literal meaning of this passage is to train up a child in *his* way. It is the child's way we are to respond to and provide appropriate training, for it will be a springboard for his success in living a fruitful and fulfilling life.

Each of us has a purpose, a gifting, a unique place in this world where we are most effective and productive. When we operate within this gifting, we feel energized and fulfilled, much the way my wife feels when she works with children and music. An activity that would deplete another's energy completely exhilarates her, as when she sees the child's pleasure at learning rhythm or singing harmony for the first time. Yes, there is the difficulty of getting and holding the attention of a group of children learning to sing together, but Jan would say, "The trouble of the present time is not worthy to be compared to the joy that is to be revealed!"[2] For when she combines music, children, and leadership, she is in her sweet spot.

It is our job as parents to help our children discover their sweet spot, their gifting, and their passion and find for them opportunities to grow in those strengths. In doing so, we fulfill the biblical instruction to train up a child according to his way.

Your children will show you their passions if you carefully watch their play. When our daughter was of elementary age, she would sit for long periods of time cutting out paper dolls and various shapes. After coloring a picture in a coloring book, Emily would carefully cut out the items in the picture with great precision. Often as we read aloud to the children, she would sit on the living room floor, doing her meticulous cutting. We thought it was just something to pass the time or keep her hands busy, or that maybe it was a "girl thing" as she was our only girl. At the age of eight, she began wanting to make her own clothes with her own designs and decorating them with cutouts appliqued on a shirt or jacket. We didn't know then, nor for many years, that these interests would one day be useful in Emily's career. Today, she is a fashion designer, cutting out intricate details that make her designs unique. When we thought she was just passing the time, she was already honing skills that would prove important to her future. Today, we laugh together as we talk about her as a young girl playing with scissors, making messes, and never being satisfied with wearing the same thing everyone else wore.

Despite not recognizing her future career track, when we saw that Emily could safely use scissors, we got rid of the schoolhouse scissors at the age of six or seven and bought her some real scissors. Children need the proper tools for success and growth, and they should have the best they can handle and the best you can afford.

None of us instantly sees the path that will become our child's life journey, but it's fun to help him find it. Without a doubt, we all have been guilty of steering our children in one direction or another according to our own desires and interests, but it is more helpful to expose them to a wide array of experiences or opportunities to "try their hand at." Piano, dance, art, drama, sports, horseback riding, hunting, fishing, construction, mechanics—be creative in finding opportunities that allow your children to explore their passions. If your daughter seems interested in animals, help her get a part-time job at a dog kennel or vet's office where she can clean cages or do the feeding and observe up close and personal a variety of animals and the people who work with them. Perhaps she can volunteer at the local zoo or an animal shelter. Living in the city is not an excuse for limiting a child's opportunities, and neither is living in the country.

This brings me to one of our family's mantras, one of the character statements we lived by as the children were growing up: *You do not find opportunity; you create it!* Create opportunities to expose your children to a variety of interests, including those you know nothing about it. People who are experts in a field love to talk about their work, especially to kids.

Finding resources is an area where my wife excelled. I made the mistake of encouraging my third son to pursue baseball and play catcher (as I had wished myself to be). All was progressing toward that end when he caught a fancy for skateboarding. I thought it would pass, but I was shocked when, at thirteen, he told me he didn't want to play ball anymore. He wanted to skate. This presented not only disappointment for me but also some obstacles for him. In the rural area where we live, there are no skate parks or facilities equipped for the exciting jumps and tricks that skateboarders love. Being an opportunist, he began building his own ramps—and then Jan intervened. You would think a mother would put a stop to such high-risk behavior, but no. She told him that if he was going to build ramps and rails for skating, he should do it well. She contacted the drafting instructor at the local technical school, who volunteered to train Rodney in drafting his designs and draw plans with precision curves for all his ramps.

You don't find opportunities, you create them.

For years, Rodney annoyed us with his daydreaming about skateboarding, running his fingers around the rim of his glass or plate as we sat at dinner. He would pretend to do jumps or tricks with his fingers on the seat beside him in the car. His consuming passion for the sport turned into a business in which he made thousands of dollars before he graduated from high school!

Suffice it to say, as you expose your children to a variety of experiences, one or two of them will stick, not because you forced it but because it was part of "the way he should go." Along the way, as you discover your child's passions and interests, you can draw upon them as a means for fostering responsibility.

Catching Your Child Doing Something Right

One of my favorite leadership books is *The One Minute Manager* by Ken Blanchard and Spencer Johnson. It's a funny little business book containing many useful insights into leading and following, but one of the most eye-opening principles presented in the book is the idea of "catching people doing something right."[3]

After assigning any new task or responsibility to an employee, the manager depicted in the book would check in more often and watch the employee more closely to confirm that he understood the new responsibility and had everything he needed to be successful. Yes, the manager was hovering, but contrary to the conventional managerial approach, the manager was not trying to catch his employee doing something wrong that he would need to step in and fix. Instead, the manager was trying to catch his employee getting it *right*. When he "caught" the employee being successful in the newly assigned role, the manager would reward him with an "Attaboy!"

When any of us begins something new, we are at our most insecure and need confirmation that at least part of what we are doing is correct. With a bit of reassurance, we become energized and motivated to keep "getting it right" and cheerfully accept additional training and practice.

So it is when our children receive a new pair of scissors, a bike, a computer, or a new task to complete. They need more focused guidance to make it clear in their minds how to be responsible with this addition. A new set of rules may help them develop the understanding and habits to manage the new situation, but remember, the rules are there for training, not to create opportunities to punish. As soon as children learn to control themselves, rules are rarely needed and freedom can prevail.

When my oldest child, Caleb, grew tall enough to reach the hanging rod in his closet, he was given responsibility for hanging up his own clothes. It was my job to train him. At first, I went with him nearly every time he put away his clothes, particularly when it involved items like long pants or collared shirts. Painstakingly, we would practice how to hold the pants by the hem with seams matching and properly creased, how to pass the hanger down the leg and fold them over. I caught him doing it right probably twenty or thirty times before I quit watching. I would praise him each time for doing it right until he learned to praise himself for his success. Soon it became an ingrained habit. Today, Caleb does a better job of hanging up his clothes than I do, but the foundation for success was laid during his elementary years.

Don't Wait Until They're Competent

It's important to note here that children should be given responsibility for a task before they are competent to complete it. Yes, I said *before*. Children have a natural passion to grow and learn, and it is the thing that is just beyond their reach that most catches their interest. Just as our horses reach their necks through the fence to eat the grass just beyond their reach while they are standing in knee-deep grass inside the fence, children want to do things that are just beyond their ability, just beyond their competence. Waiting to assign a task or give permission for an activity until they are fully competent cuts the motivation out from under them. As parents, we must listen to their driving interest and use wisdom as we let them take on a challenge and expand their skills.

Our first memorable experience with this dynamic was when our oldest child was seven or eight years old. There was a vacant lot on the corner of our street that was not being mowed regularly. Caleb had watched me mow our yard every week and thought it looked pretty easy and pretty fun. One day, he told us he wanted to mow the lot on the corner. We were shocked, but he was serious and wanted to know what would be wrong with that. We gave him a number of good reasons it was not a good idea, such as it was not our lot and he had never used a lawnmower before. But in our heads we were thinking, *You're too little!* But because he was passionately interested, Jan said to him, "You first prove to me that you can safely mow our yard with all its obstacles, and I'll consider letting you mow that lot."

Caleb, who was admittedly big for his age, took to that challenge like a dog to a bone. In the heat of a Louisiana summer, he pulled the lawnmower out and we helped him start it. We gave him some safety-related instructions, and off he went. I still remember his red, sweaty face as he proudly pushed that lawnmower up and down our yard.

With determination, he proved to us he could safely maneuver the lawnmower with reasonable precision after a just few weeks of training and close observation. He was so proud of being ready to graduate to the next level—mowing someone else's property.

The owners of the vacant lot lived in Florida, so we had to find their address and write them a letter to request permission to mow the lot, not really mentioning the age of our son. What a deal we offered them—regular upkeep of their property for just ten dollars per week! Yes, we sold our son's services. And that was the beginning of Caleb's lawn service at eight years old. He was motivated and rapidly became competent at not only mowing but also writing and sending invoices that he mailed to the property's owners for payment. Real work and real pay. He wanted the responsibility, and we were just gullible enough to let him do it. Then he trained his younger sister to be his assistant because she was champing at the bit to do what Caleb was doing. Before we knew it, they had developed a clientele with several yards within walking distance, and Jan would faithfully go to with them to make sure they remained safe.

Their success in the growing lawn business created a new opportunity to develop even more responsibility: What were they to do with all their money? Though they were in no way motivated by the money they were making, we realized this presented us an opportunity to teach our kids some money-handling skills. So Jan marched them over to the bank a block from our house and helped them apply for a business checking account. What does a bank teller say to a ten-year-old who wants to open a business account? Well, at first, nothing because she had to pick her jaw up off the floor. "Well, let's see what we need from you," she finally said. "I know who you are, but do you have any identification?"

There are some real benefits to living in a small town, especially when your family is the bunch of weirdos who homeschooled their kids before most people had heard of homeschooling. Today, a bank wouldn't allow a child to open a checking account, but the bank did that day, and the account of CHER Enterprises was created. The letters in the name signified each of our children—Caleb, Hudson, Emily, and Rodney—who would share the business profits. This account would hold the money earned from whatever they produced, and they were able to spend it on items of collective benefit approved by us. The first year, they bought new lawnmowers so they could get more yards. The following years, they bought a trampoline and an aquarium. Our children had so much fun growing in responsibility, they didn't see it as work.

Teaching Character Qualities

Early in the elementary stage, children tend to focus on physical activities like cutting, carrying, moving, and building, but equally important to their growth are skills involving the social graces. Our daughter, Emily, was physically graceful, such that she easily learned to ride a bike, balance on a board, turn somersaults, and dance. But social graces took a bit more work on her part and more grace on ours.

The tale repeatedly told in our family is the time the children were playing a board game, and all were having a great time—that is, until Emily realized she was going to lose. With great disgust, she flipped the game board into the air, scattering all the game pieces, and made some hateful remark to the other players.

With much patience from the other members of the family, we worked with Emily to manage her successes and failures, gains and losses, with grace and kindness. This involved many conversations, many comforting hugs, many apologies, and eventually, many successes along the way. We all learned together the value of speaking the truth but not necessarily saying everything that is true out loud. We learned that disappointment and failure are rarely final and that victory is indeed sweeter following a period of failure. Regardless of our circumstances, kind, genuine, and honest words are really the best.

Did you notice the significant words in this story? *Grace, truth, kindness, genuine, honest.* A child's elementary years are a time when developing character qualities becomes a significant part of training. Character is an abstract concept that children in the earlier years can only understand as actions rather than motives. The elementary stage is the time for planting concepts of character and developing basic understanding of the family's values and culture.

Children at this stage are open to accepting your values without question, so it's important to have times of discussion with them about what drives your actions and what steers your thoughts. Find short books that portray your values and use their stories as a tool for starting sincere conversations about what is important to you. Such conversations are not comfortable for everyone, so reading a book or watching a movie with a particular theme can help get the discussion started.

After a book or movie, ask questions. These can be as simple as "What did you think about the story?" or "Do you think our family is anything like that?" Then the important part begins—listening. Children perceive more than most people think, and they want to talk about it. As children open the door to discussing character traits like kindness, commitment, work ethic, or truthfulness, you will find it more comfortable to share your own thoughts about it. Discussion like this let you see the present state of your child's thoughts and feelings while also helping them fill in the gaps of their understanding.

A perfect time for character talks is bedtime. It's a magical time when children's minds and hearts are more easily opened as you make time to read, talk, and listen. It's also a great way to have some quiet time to help the kids settle down for sleep. Starting or establishing a bedtime routine is best done in the elementary years, when it is critical to begin talking about motives, values, and character.

Some parents manage to accomplish connection with their children at different times of the day, or they set aside focused time on the weekend for heart chats. Find what works for you and do it as often as possible because this the time that a great preacher of old, Charles Spurgeon, spoke of when he said, "You must stack the wood on the altar of their hearts, so that when the Spirit of God sets fire to their passion, there will be wood to burn."

We can't force our children to become people of good character, but we can talk of it and live it before them, establishing for them a framework for understanding what good character looks like, feels like, and acts like.

Learn to Ask Open-Ended Questions

Learning to connect with your child in conversation is essential to passing on the values you possess. Though you can live out your values in view of your child, he or she will not fully understand your reasoning until you explain *why* you live the way you do. Learning to engage children in a conversation that enables them to truly understand is one of the core skills of parenting. Your success in this area hinges not on making profound statements full of wisdom and truth but, rather, on asking questions that open your child's mind. Thus, an essential skill for every parent is the ability to ask open-ended questions.

What is an open-ended question? It's a question that can only be answered by one or more sentences. For instance, "Did you have a good time at the party?" is not open-ended because it's answerable with a one-word response like "Yes," "No," or "Kinda." Instead, maybe ask, "How did it go at the party?" or say, "Tell me about something you liked or disliked at the party."

Even though I have practiced this for years, it still takes effort to ask questions that allow you to hear the thoughts, feelings, and values of another person. But once the flow of words begins, your most important job is to really listen to what's being said, and that goes beyond the words. As we listen to the words, other questions should come to mind that will help the person elaborate on what he or she thinks or feels about the subject of the conversation.

In the example of asking about a party your daughter attended, she might mention in passing that someone was mean, or something surprised her, or that she wanted something different. These are little windows into the feelings and desires that should prompt another question like "What was mean about that person?" or "What did you expect?" or maybe "What were you hoping for?"

Children want to be understood, and they know the difference between when someone is really interested and when someone is just asking questions. So it's important that you really want to hear their thoughts and feelings before giving them a lecture about your thoughts and feelings. When kids feel understood, they are better able to listen to another person's perspective.

"Do you want to know what Daddy thinks about that situation?" you might ask at some point. Asking permission to speak is not required, but it often helps the child to receive input from the parent without feeling condemned or corrected. It also gives her a moment and cue to shift mentally from talking about herself to listening to another.

When seeking to explain why you live out your values a certain way, opening with a question is also good. For example, "Do you know why I made you stay with the grocery cart today while I stepped away to talk with the lady at the end of the aisle?" or "Do you know why I got so angry when you knocked over the plant?"

Once you have a sense that the child is listening, the opportunity has arrived for you to explain why things are a certain way, why you value certain character traits, or why you live, act, or speak a certain way. This is also a time to explain that other people are different and how your family will respond to those differences. It's also the time to find the good character behind the feelings they're describing and praise those traits.

Building Respect

During our children's elementary years, we must foster the development of responsibility and character. As we do, we will take giant steps forward in the pursuit of an influential relationship, shifting from control to a better, more comfortable, and effective place for both parent and child.

As you seek to increase your influence with your child, trust in the relationship must continually grow. But as you think of trust, consider that the core component of trust is respect. Respect is that sense that "I am valued, and someone is interested in me." Even with children, respect must be a two-way street. They respect you, and you respect them. This is one reason I often suggest that parents ask permission to give their opinion to the child. The show of respect helps the child to be able to hear the opinion another person.

The elementary years are mostly about building competence with skills, but it's also the best time to build a habit of engaging in respect-filled conversations, because the emotional volatility of the tween years it a difficult stage in which to work on it. And those tween years are the subject of the next chapter.

CHAPTER 9

Changes in Latitude,
Changes in Attitude

Reducing the Turbulence of the Tween Years

The ages between ten and thirteen are crisis years that set the stage for coming adolescence. The "turbulent tweens" will challenge your sanity as a parent as, before your very eyes, your wonderful child will appear to unravel and/or undergo a personality change. Your preteen may appear to lose his or her mind, taking yours with it. Yet the turbulence you see during this period is nothing compared to what your child feels happening inside his or her brain and body.

Let me begin by recommending a great resource that explains what is happening both emotionally and developmentally in the body, mind, and soul of your preteen. *No Longer Little* by Hal and Melanie Young is well researched, well written, and full of guidance for understanding this transitional time in the lives of our tweens.[1] I leaned on the Youngs' wisdom while writing this chapter, so if you are the parent of a child in this stage, I encourage you to explore this subject further in their book. *No Longer Little* will help you better grasp the reasoning behind much of the practical application we will discuss over the next several pages. It's a comforting, lighthearted book that will help you to stay the course and not lose heart when your preteen has an emotional meltdown or simply appears to be "off in another world."

Another excellent resource I recommend is Dr. James Dobson's *Bringing Up Boys*, which addresses some of the neurobiology of the preteen brain and its transformation.[2] His focus is on how the brains of boys are physically and functionally different from those of girls due largely to hormonal influences. Though Dr. Dobson is writing about raising boys, his book is a good introduction to the physiology behind the bewildering childhood behaviors and thoughts we often see at this age. This is not to say that biology is an excuse for unacceptable behavior, but it can help us to understand why some things may be more of a struggle for one gender or the other, or for one age group or another.

The Waltz in Swing Time

As children transition from one developmental stage to the next—each on his or her own unique timetable—they experience changes in brain function that require significant adjustment. During the elementary years, when our children's progression was about learning responsibility, much of their character training looked like physical work—picking up toys, hanging up clothes, buckling seatbelts, helping in the kitchen, and so on. Having "mastered" the physical aspects of responsibility training, preteens now begin to focus on the *feelings* they have toward responsibility.

Thus begin the swings of emotion that cause so much distress for parents at this stage. Tweens' moods become mercurial, suddenly and unexpectedly shifting from highly excited to deeply depressed (or vice versa) about issues that appear rather mundane to the rest of us. Even the most responsible and compliant child may become emotionally volatile, exploding into tears of frustration over simple decisions like which shoes to wear or what a friend meant when he spoke to another person in her hearing.

As many of us parents grew up, it was this period of emotional turbulence that resulted in so many of our painful memories. That's because everything at this stage was wrapped in emotions. Feelings came alive for us, coloring our experiences both with vibrant hues and deep dark shades, just as they will for your child. It's this stage of development my wife refers to when she says, "Who in his right mind would want to go back to junior high?!?"

Likewise, your child's preteen years will be a time of learning how the emotions of life fit with the construct of responsibility, character, and relationships they formed in the elementary years. Everything begins to look different to the preteen because it all *feels* different. These new feelings cause tweens to question the validity of their prior experience and so reevaluate the trustworthiness of their thoughts. Things they previously accepted from their parents with "the faith of a child" now may be given a second thought, especially when the tween's thoughts and feelings don't match.

Common statements made by preteens include "I don't feel like it," "I'm too tired," "I'm so excited," and "I'm afraid to." Notice how the language of emotion is coming to the forefront, replacing the "I want to" of the elementary years with words that communicate feelings. The feelings they're experiencing now tend to be the focus of thoughts and greatly distract them from previously learned habits of responsibility and obedience.

Many parents of preteens describe them as "walking around in a fog." This fog is created by new emotions and appetites that begin before the physical changes of puberty set in. That's what makes this stage so difficult for parents—the child's body looks much the same, but inside, the mind and emotions are roiling, causing behavior to change.

For parents, it's tempting to interpret our tween's new emotional language as whining or complaining and so respond to it with emotions of our own, adding fuel to the fire within the child. This validates for the child his sense that this new emotional world he's discovered is not a safe one. It's as if the preteen has awakened to find himself in a dream state where all the rules of engagement have changed, and now he's just trying to figure out how to get along. When he tries to communicate his thoughts or feelings, he is constantly reading the listener for understanding and acceptance. If the child receives a negative response every time he expresses himself, this will cause him to withdraw and cease communicating openly.

Creating a Safe Environment for Your Tween

Just as a turtle in a shell first sticks its head out to see if it's safe but draws quickly back into its shell at any sign of a threat, a child who feels unsafe will pull back into herself, where she will then brood over slights that may or may not be real but which she perceived. Our job as parents during this phase is to create an emotionally safe environment so the preteen will stick her neck out and let us see what is going on inside the shell. Only then can we help her make sense of her inner world and help her relate to the world around her.

This is when you will begin to catch glimpses of the mature person your child is becoming. Because this stage is critical to the emotional health that will eventually enable her to soar in life, it's important for you now to be present physically, emotionally, and spiritually for your child. That's because you are her measuring stick for what is okay. If she senses your acceptance, that's good; if she senses your rejection, that's bad.

Granted, it's difficult to find a happy medium in how you respond in each interaction with your preteen. The behavior and attitudes you're seeing may not be at all acceptable, and you might find you don't particularly *like* the new version of this child. But you must learn to communicate acceptance to her while not condoning wrong actions and attitudes.

Of course, you will find it helpful if you're emotionally healthy enough yourself to give room for your tween's emotional expression. As she grows and matures, mistakes and blunders will be part of her process. Just as we experienced during our own growing up, she will feel awkward and unacceptable, which is so easily interpreted as rejection. This makes everyone a bit uncomfortable. But we should take heart from John Maxwell's adage that no one grows in the comfort zone, and get comfortable being uncomfortable.

It's helpful to have a dose of compassion ready to administer to your child during her preteen years. Kindness and understanding are like a glue for binding your child's heart to yours. Indeed, applying large doses of kindness will be vital during this stage. If you have wisely built a foundation of trust in the earlier years, rest upon it in turbulent moments, knowing that your preteen is actually more upset with herself than with you and that her maturity level may be limiting her ability to communicate this to you. If you feel rejected by her, understand that it may really be a reflection of your child's own inner struggle with feelings of rejection. Avoiding taking a defensive posture with your preteen during this time is very important to developing a relationship of influence in the coming years.

Now Is the Time to Begin Yielding Control

The tween years are when parenting gets a little scary. Maybe it's the very reason you picked up this book. You realize you're beginning to lose control, and this feels abnormal and wrong because it's a whole new experience in your parenting journey.

Rest assured that losing control is a natural and necessary part of shepherding your child toward adulthood. Now that your child is a preteen, it's your job to help him learn to manage the control he has wanted and is now terrified he has. Once you understand this, you can learn to control your own fears and frustrations and be a great help to your transitioning preteen.

Let's take another look at the graph depicting the shift parents must make to remain effective in preparing their child for life as an adult. As shown in figure 3, parental control is rapidly declining during the preteen phase. Keep in mind, this is not caused by poor parenting or childhood rebellion but is a function of maturing. Inside, the child is changing before we can see or measure the bodily change that is coming. Trying to hold on to control as a parent during this developmental stage is like trying to hold back a tidal wave with a Dixie cup. No one wins in those situations.

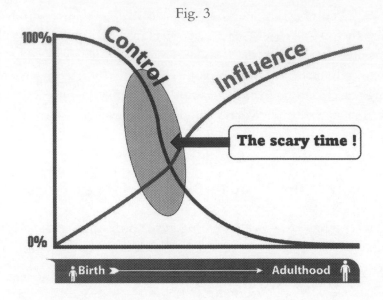

Fig. 3

To win as a family, parents must begin making the necessary shift toward influence by yielding control to the child at this stage, maybe even handing it off as quickly as possible.

Lewis Hershey, a four-star general in the U.S. Army who was director of the Selective Service for almost three decades, captured the tension in this process of transferring control when he said, "A boy becomes an adult three years before his parents think he does, and two years after he thinks he does."[3] It is important that we not undershoot in setting expectations for our children's progression to maturity. It is much better for them to have to stretch to attain to our high estimation of them rather than stooping to meet our low estimation.

Let's begin turning our attention now to some practical steps for training preteens to handle their increasing control.

Learning from Natural Consequences

A principle that is often lost in our present culture is the link between freedom and responsibility. As freedom increases, so does responsibility. Training preteens to understand and internalize this principle will be key to their success in subsequent stages of life. If a clear connection is made between freedom and responsibility, a child's progress toward maturity can be astounding.

It's one thing for a child to give verbal ascent to the idea that freedom brings responsibility, but it is altogether another thing to have experienced it and learned it from the School of Hard Knocks. This school is what I refer to as *natural consequences.*

Far too often, parents respond to a child's irresponsible actions by contriving a knee-jerk penalty that is completely unrelated to the issue. Consider, for example, the old standby, grounding. What real-life connection is there between the child's use of a smartphone and his harshness toward a sibling? Or between getting to go to a concert and leaving the milk out of the refrigerator?

I'm not saying a parent can't use a privilege to reward some unrelated responsible action. That's different from becoming aggravated over an action or attitude and pronouncing, "That's it! You're grounded! You're not going to that birthday party tomorrow!" There is a lot wrong with this picture. Sudden anger. High volume. Unrelated consequence.

It's also likely the parent waited too long to intervene in the situation. Waiting too long to address a child's error often results in a parental explosion, thus creating an emotionally unsafe environment. The whole atmosphere becomes tense such that the spouse falls silent, the siblings are frozen, and even the dog looks guilty. Everyone feels unsafe.

While this picture may accurately represent the way you or your spouse was raised, it's far from desirable. Just because it was part of the past doesn't mean it has to be part of your family's present or future.

As a parent, you have the opportunity to create a heathy, safe environment in your home by working hard at communicating acceptance and value to your children and patiently training them in responsibility. You can make huge strides in this area by proactively seeking to grow in your understanding of each child and his or her unique complexities. The very fact that you are reading this book is evidence that you are willing and desirous of change. Kudos!

So what does it look like to use natural consequences as a teaching tool?

I'm simply talking about letting your child suffer the effects of a bad decision he or she has made. Now, this approach can seem unkind or harsh at times, but it doesn't have to be mean. It takes a lot of strength and courage on the part of a parent to let a child dig himself into a hole and then let him stay there until he remedies the situation. Often, the parent suffers as much as the child, but it's not without purpose.

Proper use of consequences will teach a child to change his behavior, initially to avoid the ramifications but eventually because he will reach the conclusion on his own that *there is a better way.* As he counsels himself based on his negative experience—and perhaps even *seek* advice from his parents—he will begin to grow in the area of self-control. And that, ladies and gentlemen, is the key to eliminating your child's need for you.

Here are a few practical examples of natural consequences in the preteen years:

- Your daughter refuses to take a heavy coat with her on a cold day as you advise. Later, when she realizes the thin sweater she's wearing isn't warm enough, she calls home and pleads for someone to bring her a coat, but no one is available.
- Your son forgets to take a lunch to school and must therefore go hungry for the day.
- Your daughter forgets to put her soccer uniform in the wash or hang it up to prevent winkling. Then she has a choice—miss the game or wear the uniform as is, much to her embarrassment (and yours).
- Your son leaves his bicycle on the front lawn where it is stolen in the night, and he misses many opportunities to ride with friends.

It can be tricky giving advice, sometimes knowing your child will reject it, but then letting the situation play out. Granted, I'm not talking about issues that are fatal or dangerous. They may, however, prove to be uncomfortable and even embarrassing. If so, offer your support and guidance while giving the child just a little more control than she can handle so she is constantly stretching herself and occasionally surprising the both of you. It is imperative, however, that you resist the urge to say "I told you so." Instead, a good response may something as simple as a compassionate "I'm sorry it turned out that way." Or maybe, "What would you like to do differently next time?"

One of my favorite stories from a fellow horse trainer involves a nine- or ten year-old boy who came to his farm to live and work as part of a program to help the child mature. As I recall, this was a foster child who had very little training in responsibility and character. He was assigned a horse to care for, and it was his responsibility to see that the horse had food and water every day.

The boy forgot to water the horse two days in a row before it was discovered that the horse was dehydrated and weak. The boy was shown the results of his irresponsibility and was assigned the solution. Because the horse would drink itself sick if given free access to water, the boy was given a cup with which he was to carry water from the faucet fifty feet to the horse's bucket, time after time, until the water overflowed the bucket and dripped on the ground. He was not allowed to stop or come in for supper until the job was complete. This was important for the health of the horse, and it was also important for the growth of the boy.

As the boy retrieved cup after cup and poured it into the bucket, the water was immediately lapped up by the parched animal. After more than an hour, only a small amount of water had accumulated in the bottom of the bucket. It was long after dark before the horse was satisfied enough to step away from the bucket, and it was late into the night before the first drop spilled over onto the ground. At this point, the exhausted boy was congratulated for a job well done and welcomed into the house where his supper awaited him.

The boy learned his lesson well that day not because he was punished, but because he experienced the natural consequences of letting his horse become dehydrated. No one had to shout at him or issue threats. They just had to get out of his way while he did what was right.

After that day, no one had to remind the boy to take care of his horse or to think of its needs before his own. Days and weeks went by, and the mistake was never mentioned again. But the lesson was never forgotten. A change had taken place in the boy's mind and heart that day as he stared into the blank eyes of a dehydrated animal that was sick because of his neglect and carelessness. And this change was reinforced each day when he was met with the glistening eyes of an excited horse receiving food and water from the now-responsible boy.

It's great when situations present such clear natural consequences, but honestly, more times than not, we have to help make some associations for our children. This must not be a knee-jerk retaliatory response but, rather, a lesson that is carefully planned and communicated. It must be clear to all involved 1) what is the expected behavior or action, and 2) what will be granted or denied as a result.

For example, with four active children in our home, there was no shortage of "stuff." There came a day when as I walked through the house, I kept having to step over articles of clothing, ball gloves, hats, toys, books, purses—STUFF! This had to stop, and I had to stop it. But how?

At that time, our children were involved in horse show competitions, which means we had acquired a great many things made of leather— saddles, bridles, halters, spur straps, and the like. Leather must be conditioned regularly to remain supple and prevent cracking. Therein was part of the solution. Work needed to be done, *and* I wanted the children to pick up their stuff without being reminded. So we came up with a plan to associate an undesirable action with work that everyone knew needed to be done but no one wanted to do.

I got a big cardboard box to serve as my "jail" for items left on the floor. Anytime, day or night, I could pass through the house and collect anything left on the floor and put it in the cardboard jail. The owner of each item could either lose it or redeem it. It mattered not to me which way they chose, and I did not let emotion enter into the deal. If someone desired to redeem an article, he or she had to apply conditioner to one item of leather. We usually would let the child do the conditioning while we read books aloud or watched a television program as a family. This approach was most effective when a favorite pair of shorts, a Sunday shoe, or a ball glove was at stake. When I incarcerated their stuff, the kids knew they had caused their own problem, and little by little, they improved their ways. Never was it perfect, but we weren't aiming for perfection. Jan and I were satisfied to see the growth of responsible habits without resorting to a lot of shouting.

This approach would not have worked if I had furiously stomped through the house, picking up the kids' stuff for them, or if I had tried to humiliate them when they failed to put things away. Oh, there were probably times when Jan announced my imminent arrival with a reminder to "pick up your things." All I know is that the house began to feel better, the leather looked better, and I felt better. And so did the kids, who were developing some good habits.

Celebrate Attempts and Successes

Children really *want* to grow and mature, and we can help them by celebrating their attempts as well as their successes. We should look for opportunities for them to exert some control over their world by giving them real "adult" responsibilities and expecting them to make a difference in the family by following through. When they fail, we all fail with them. Successes and failures become smaller issues if we determine we're all going to remain on the same team and avoid the "blame game." Our kids need to see that taking the journey together is its own reward.

Preteen children can be given responsibility for preparing a family meal, maybe with the help of an older sibling, parent, or babysitter. The meal is then eaten by everyone whether it's good or not. The goal is to experience a "win" as often as possible, but when things don't work out so well, everyone endures it together. At least, that's the goal. Yes, siblings may have a hard time holding their tongues when the meal is not to their liking. But they also know their turn is coming, and they may need others to extend grace to them too.

Some responsibilities are simply fun for children, such as when my wife would pull into a gas station for refueling. Our children would negotiate among themselves to decide who pumped the gas, who washed the windshield, and eventually, who checked the oil. Jan never left her seat while the busy little bees did their work. Naturally, we had to train the oldest child to operate the pump safely, but we really only had to train the one. The first one then trained the others as they were able to handle the task. The untrained kids got to squeegee the windshield. Sometimes, it looked rather streaky afterward, but this exercise wasn't about having a spotless windshield; it was about allowing the children to be cheerfully responsible to the level of their ability.

Allowing or requiring kids to manage money is also great training for the future. They will need all the practice they can get in the area of budgeting and decision-making. While helping with the shopping, children can try to find the best deals on the grocery list or see who can gather all the things on their portion of the list and return to the cart the quickest. Or they can learn to compare quality and prices of things at a secondhand store versus buying new. The next step is allowing them to actually make the choices as to what to buy with the money allowed for their clothing purchases. Children want to participate in adult decisions, and we must train them to make those decisions as if we weren't there. Why? Because the goal of parenting is to eliminate our children's need for us.

Of course, children at this stage will begin to want control of more than money and a few responsibilities. They will also want to control their time, and they will be vocal about it. Emotional outbursts and passionate pleas are not uncommon when preteens are denied control over their time.

"Why *can't* I go on the youth trip?!"

"Why do I have to get up *now*?!"

"But I *want* to join the soccer team!"

As parents, we must develop thick skin to ward off the fiery darts sometimes loosed by angry preteens during this stage. These are prime training moments that will test our finesse at managing our own emotions in response. We might be justified in feeling righteous indignation at our child's brazen lack of respect, but we must remind ourselves that parenting is not about *us*. As John Maxwell has said, "To handle yourself, you should use your head. But to handle others, you should use your heart."[4] We must be prepared to manage ourselves and practice restraint during an unfair attack while also having compassion for our hormone-addled preteen.

A humorous but coarse book about life as a medical resident was circulating during my residency years. Though I never read it, its subject matter was widely discussed among my peers as we endured the grind of residency. Quotes from the book brought a bit of levity to our tired, depleted existence as medical residents. One such quote addressed emergency situations such as when a patient collapsed or was found unresponsive. A "Code Blue" went out, and we would race up flights of stairs and down long halls before arriving breathlessly at the scene of the emergency. The book's advice in this situation was simple: "First, check your own pulse!" It's funny but true that we were not going to be much help to others until we first regained our composure. Airline safety instructions put it like this: "First put on your own oxygen mask before assisting others."

So it is with parents and the surge of emotions—if your emotions are running high, you're not likely to be much use in helping your child. When tempers flare in a confrontation between parent and preteen, we must be the more mature ones and deny ourselves the urge to "flame on" and burn our opponent. We must learn to set aside our own feelings to help our distressed child manage the turmoil he or she is dealing with inside.

Please don't misunderstand me on this point. I'm not saying you shouldn't address disrespectful behavior. Nor am I making excuses for a child who's being obnoxious. What I am saying is to respectfully understand your child's inner turmoil and her inexperience in communicating her thoughts and feelings.

We must train our preteens to rein in these emotions that signal a need for change or the pain of losing something. Society's pattern for communicating in times of disappointment is to get loud, get proud. But that works poorly between individuals, especially in a family. We need to help our preteens to calm down and tell us what they are wanting and feeling and maybe even why, if they can find the words to express it.

Next time your tween goes ballistic on you, try communicating something like this:

> "Honey, come here and talk to me about what's upsetting you so much about this situation. I want to understand you clearly. It would help me to hear if you'll sit down with me and use a quieter voice. There may be something I don't know about this issue, and I want to understand."

The words you use may be different, but the message should be the same: *I want to know you. I want to help you. Please talk to me.*

Perhaps right now you're saying, "But my child won't listen to me!"

That is the opposite of what I am saying.

YOU need to listen to THEM.

For only when preteens feel understood are they able to hear what you are saying. This principle is one of the habits described in Steven Covey's bestselling book *The Seven Habits of Highly Effective People.*[5]

Habit 5 is:

Seek first to understand, *then* to be understood.

Parents would do well to develop this habit and practice it during the preteen and teen years if they want to make the necessary shift from control to influence in the lives of their children.

Seeking to understand someone involves remaining calm, asking questions, and listening to the answers in such a way that you hear the heart of what is said. Avoid questions that are accusatory, as in "What did you mean by that, young lady?!?" Instead, lovingly say, "Help me to understand what you meant when you said [fill in the blank]."

Our own experience as adults should tell us that it's much easier to accept an answer we dislike when we feel our position has been heard and completely understood. Although we may be disappointed with the decision, we are able to process the fact that there are other valid opinions and we cannot change the situation right now. You have the privilege of helping your preteen begin to experience this concept when there is a clear "no" to her request. Helping her respectfully express her desires and disappointments in the situation is helping her take a giant step forward toward maturity.

A Couple of Caveats

So much wisdom is needed as we train our preteens in the area of communication. In the pre-computer age, there was room for error that's not afforded to kids today. As recently as the 1980s, if a preteen spoke disrespectfully to his parent or let his emotions get the better of him, the parent handled it in one way or another, either effectively or not, but eventually the child matured and improved in his communication. Past indiscretions were largely forgotten.

Not so today. Passionate diatribes are recorded for posterity in social media posts and shared with all the world within a matter of moments. Today, just ignoring irresponsible or disrespectful communication is like hating your own children and can lead to their destruction. It's critical that we address virulent patterns of communication quickly and effectively—not by suppressing our children's expression but with training that teaches them how to use their freedom wisely.

Social media, regardless of the platform, has brought a whole new level of complexity to communication training and management. Whole books are devoted to navigating this minefield, so suffice it to say, my comments here will be incomplete. But an underlying principle to keep in mind is the need for continued building of trust and open communication between the parent and child. During the Cold War era, President Ronald Reagan often quoted a Russian proverb that goes, "Trust, but verify." This goes for the parent-child relationship as well.

Remember, relationship math tells us that resentment and rebellion result from a situation where rules and regulations are emphasized out of balance with relationship. The relationship is the variable in the balance of this equation. The healthier the relationship, the less likely it is that resentment and rebellion will occur. As you now know, in the preteen stage, the power of the parent-child relationship is wrapped up in the child's feeling understood, truly known, and accepted. You've also learned that working on this relationship means training, coaching, listening, and checking your own pulse regularly—all with the goal of transferring control to your maturing child while shifting the emphasis to your influence and the child's freedom.

A word of caution: Although freedom is a wonderful thing, it can be quite unsettling at first. When an animal is let out of its cage, it usually becomes hyperactive and excited. Although my wife doesn't like it much when I do it, I will sometimes open the gate to our horse pastures and leave it open without the horses being aware. When they finally discover their newfound freedom, the animals get all excited and prance around for a few minutes. If I were to try in this moment to restrain them and get them immediately back into their pen, the horses would run from me like a gang of bandits. But if I just wait a bit and act like I'm not concerned about them, they soon settle down and go back to eating grass. That's when I walk up to them, casually slip a loose rope around their necks, and then lead them back to within their safe boundaries. Of course, children are not horses, and this is not a perfect illustration of the situation we face as parents. But it does show that freedom is not very comfortable for anyone at first. Your children need you to give them freedom, and then they need you to guide them in freedom.

When you tell someone you have a child about to become a teenager, they may cry, "I am so sorry!" while comforting you and reminding you that this too shall pass. I say that's nonsense! The teen years can be the best years of parenthood if you have not resisted the transfer of control to your preteen but have instead invested well in an open, trusting, communicative relationship that has allowed the child to experience both successes and failures in handling control under your watchful and compassionate eye. The child's experience with managing some freedom in this phase will prepare the child (and you) for the exciting teen years where a beautiful flower can then bloom—the flower of self-control. If you can manage this transition well, you will have no reason to dread the teen years. Indeed, you may be in for a treat!

CHAPTER 10

The Spring of Hope

Reaping the Benefits in the Teen Years

STOP. If you have jumped ahead to this chapter because you are in desperate need of help with an out-of-control teen, I feel your pain, and I will offer some solutions in the next couple of chapters. I urge you, however, to back up and read chapter nine, for you are going need principles and strategies from the preteen chapter to break down some walls and build bridges with your teen. Without them, what I am about to propose may seem unrealistic.

In this chapter and the next, we're going to discuss several loaded topics such as driving, dating, curfews, phones, money, and plans for the future—subjects which in many homes lead to shouting, hateful stares, and coarse gestures. Believe me, I've seen it all in my career as a physician and counselor. I have treated both parents and teens for physical injuries resulting from "disagreements." I have worked with runaways and walkaways. I've seen conflict between parents and teens lead to anxiety, depression, and even suicide.

And yet I am convinced that the teen years can be the best, most fulfilling time in the relationship between a parent and child.

The Best of Times or Worst of Times?

So why then do we hear so often about parents struggling with their teens and fending off all-out rebellion? Well, common results are usually due to common methods. And I get it. There's much comfort in traveling a common path. We see many others taking the same route, and we reason it must be safe. Right?

And so, like canoes adrift on a quiet stream, we float along through the early years and elementary years, thinking, *This parenting thing isn't so hard.* Oh, there's the occasional obstacle or unexpected bend, but we develop confidence as we make the necessary adjustments and continue to go with the flow.

But then, almost imperceptibly at first, the river picks up pace.

As our children enter the preteen years, the water moves faster and faster, and bewildering rapids soon appear. We take a few bumps and bruises at this stage, and yet as the hazards increase, most of us inexplicably fail to change course or at the very least stop, rest, and reevaluate our direction and approach. Then suddenly, the teen years are upon us, and we find ourselves paddling madly, steering in vain as the cultural and developmental currents drive us this way and that, down eddies and falls, dashing our hull against massive boulders, fallen trees, and submerged, unseen dangers.

At this point, all we can do is hope that everything turns out all right.

Right?

Wrong.

Just holding on and wishing for the best is not a very good strategy for navigating a river, and it's certainly a poor approach to raising kids.

Admittedly, the teen years can be an adventure for both parent and child. Charles Dickens wasn't writing about adolescence in *A Tale of Two Cities*, but he could have been:

> *It was the best of times, it was the worst of times,*
> *it was the age of wisdom, it was the age of foolishness,*
> *it was the epoch of belief, it was the epoch of incredulity,*
> *it was the season of Light, it was the season of Darkness,*
> *it was the spring of hope, it was the winter of despair . . .*

Even in the best of situations—with the wisest of parents—things can happen that are outside of your control (and your child's) that may result in a "winter of despair." However, because these things are beyond your control, we will focus here on those things you can and should be affecting.

But know this: There's nothing common about the parenting path I'm laying out for you.

Taking *this* path requires planning, foresight, and courage.

A strategic parent will look ahead to discover where the treacherous parts are and then determine the best means of navigation, whether it's to keep right, keep left, or climb out of the stream altogether and carry the canoe over a rocky path, past the danger, and down to the next pool stage. As with many rapids, sometimes it's best to aim straight for the heart of an issue, while other times it's better to steer toward the path of least turbulence or avoid dangerous risks completely by choosing a different route.

Now, I'm not at all saying you must raise your children the way Jan and I raised ours. But you can take a lot of the guesswork and fear out of parenting by recognizing and responding to a clear progression in the development of your children, with each step setting the stage for the next.

Experience and the Path to Wisdom

How does one find success in any undertaking?

"Wisdom," said the expert to his business students when asked for the secret to his great success in business.

"How did you get wisdom?" they responded.

"That's simple, my friends: By doing things right."

"How did you learn to do things right?"

"That's simple, my friends: By gaining experience."

"How did you gain experience?"

"That's simple, my friends: By doing things wrong."

Making mistakes is one path to wisdom, or at least the path to experience. But it's not the path I recommend, for the cost is quite high and the results are not always good or dependable.

There's an old saying that goes, "A smart man is one who learns from his mistakes, but a genius is one who learns from the mistakes of others." Parents should be more than smart; they should be geniuses. Genius parents watch the "practice runs" of others who go before them so they can anticipate trouble spots and challenges (as well as periods of rest).

The first time I ever played golf, I participated in a charity golf scramble. I didn't understand what a scramble was when I signed up, but I quickly realized that the teams were amassing incredible scores compared to those I see posted by professional golfers on TV. I only knew that the event organizers had tried to balance out the teams so that each one had an A, B, C, and D player, placed according to skill level.

Most golf scrambles work like this: At every hole, each of the four team members hits a tee shot. The team then collectively decides which of the four balls is in the most advantageous position. After the team decides which ball is best, each player retrieves his ball (if it's still retrievable) and plays his next shot from the chosen position. This procedure is repeated after each shot until the team has holed one of their balls.

The team I played for settled on a strategy of having our weakest player hit first, then progressing upward so that our most skilled player hit last. Every time a player struck his ball, the next golfer watched what happened, thus learning information about how to approach the same shot when it was his turn. Each team member learned from the successes and failures of those who went before him. In this way, we scored remarkably well because of the collective wisdom we gained by playing together. None of us could have shot an individual score equal to the team's effort had he played alone.

In the same way, we can better navigate the course of parenting by learning from the successes and failures of those who go ahead of us. Sometimes, at first, we only have an opportunity to observe D-level parents, in which case we need to learn from their mistakes. But as we go along in our parenting journey, we will get to observe more skillful parents, and we can learn from both their mistakes and successes.

Regardless of where we start out, there are ways to grow and learn from the wisdom and experience of others, and we can stand on their shoulders to reach higher for the benefit of our children. I sought to do a better job than my parents, and I hope my children do a better job than I did. But the only way that will happen is if change occurs. If we merely mimic what we have seen other parents do, we're likely to make many of the same mistakes. Carefully, we need to modify or eliminate the weak practices and choices of others if we hope to achieve better results.

Of course, we also need to recognize our own mistakes and shortcomings and learn from them, attempting to do better every day. But for you and me to get better, we must be willing to change. So here we go.

How to Build Trust with Your Teen

As kids transition into adolescence, they start wanting to talk about "adult" things. Certainly, most teens are capable of holding an adult conversation. The term "adult conversation" may bring to mind intimate topics, but I'm talking about something bigger than sex or gossip. I'm referring to the meaty discussion that's triggered by the question *Why?* Not as in "Why can't I go to the movie?" or "Why do I have to study?" but real, serious questions from a young person seeking answers to life's most difficult issues.

"Why is there so much hatred in the world?"

"Why do people believe the climate is (or is not) changing?"

"Why does our neighbor collect things for the homeless shelter?"

"Why is there still hunger in the world if we can produce so much food?"

"Why do bad things happen to good people?"

"Why am I so different from everyone else?"

"Why do I feel like a failure?"

Every child is different, but somewhere during the tween and teen years, kid's minds begin to turn from the question of *how* things work to the issue of *why* things work (or don't work).

By the time they're teens, kids have developed many areas of competence. Teens generally have access to a wide vocabulary and many stories. They likely know a lot about music, media, technology, and social behaviors. Their experiences and interests will have given them knowledge in a variety of areas such as food, art, crafts, fashion, sports, dance, exercise, books, performing arts, religion, animal care, or fishing. At times they are experts in a particular area; at other times they only perceive themselves to be experts. Regardless, they are entering a phase of wanting to talk about what they know.

At the same time, they begin looking for answers to questions of why, and it's vitally important that the person your teen wants to ask these questions of is you. If you are not your teen's go-to person for finding real answers, that should tell you there is urgent work you need to do toward building, or rebuilding, your relationship.

People go to their most trusted source for information. The key word here is *trusted*. What is it that makes a person worthy of your child's trust? If you don't figure out the answer to that question, your time as the parent of a teen will be fraught with heartache, tears, and sleepless nights.

The key to fostering trust in your teen is building trust into your relationship. And yet, people don't really trust a relationship; they trust a person. To build a trusting relationship with your teen, you must show yourself to be a person worthy of his or her trust. Trust must be earned.

Sure, we'd all like to think we've banked some trust with our children after everything we've done for them over the last dozen or so years, not to mention all the anguish we've experienced on their behalf. So when our teens throw a little side-eye our way, it's tempting to get all offended and launch into a lecture about how they owe us respect. But demanding trust disqualifies you in the eyes of your teen. You can only earn or strengthen trust if particular trust-worthy traits are known to be true about you and if these traits characterize the interactions with your teen.

What are these traits?

Four words describe the type of person who is worthy of trust:

- care
- character
- competence
- consistency

These are the characteristics that will either foster trust in a relationship or, where they are lacking, prevent it. Let's examine these one at a time.

Caring

John Maxwell is an expert on leadership. Because parenting is leadership, most of his teachings apply directly to managing a home and family. One of Maxwell's favorite sayings is "People don't care how much you know until they know how much you care."[1]

The degree to which you genuinely care about your child will deeply affect your child's growth and development. However, it is also true that it doesn't matter how much you care if the child does not know it. As we discussed in chapter six, you must communicate with your child in such a way that your love and concern are clearly received. Let's face it, we often send confusing signals to our teens, especially when we're stressed. In fact, it often seems that teens and parents are speaking different languages, resulting in both parties sending offensive or misunderstood messages. I'm not speaking here of words formed with our mouths but, rather, the different ways we attempt to express love without words.

In his book *The Five Love Languages,* Gary Chapman describes five general ways people send—and receive—expressions of love.[2] If you are unfamiliar with Dr. Chapman's work, it is essential that you read it, listen to it, or watch a YouTube video of someone explaining it. These five "languages" are core to understanding so much of the disconnect that can happen between a parent and child.

Numerous family relationships have been disrupted (or worse) simply because one person was seeking to say "I love you" with one language while the recipient was listening with another language and interpreted what was said very differently. This concept of love languages applies to all relationships, not just the parent–child relationship, and recognizing when this is happening in your home can be a huge step toward identifying and breaking down barriers between family members. If you or your spouse has a strong sense that your child does not feel loved by you, now is the time to stop and gain some understanding of love languages.

Building bridges to your teen is necessary if he or she is ever to have trust. Without trust, communication between you and your teen will never flow freely. As parent, it is your job to be the bridge builder, and the first bridge to building trust is caring and effectively communicating that you care.

Character

The second bridge to building trust is character. It's said that Abraham Lincoln mused, "Perhaps a man's character [is] like a tree, and his reputation like its shadow. The shadow is what we think of it; the tree is the real thing."[3] Many people may know your reputation, but that holds no water with your children. They're watching you in good times and bad, when life is easy and when it's hard. They know the real you and are not deceived by the size of your shadow.

If your character is indeed good, your kids are not concerned with others' opinions of you. And if your character is bad, they are even less concerned with others' opinions of you. They know the truth even when you try to paint a different picture for them. If the quality of your character is an issue, no amount of parenting advice or coaching is going to mend your family. *You* have to be mended. The quality of your character will be the measure of the quality children will find in relationship with you. It's a humbling thought but true.

One day, when our middle son was in his early teens, tensions were high between him and his mother. He was quite irritable about everything. Finally, Jan asked him directly what was wrong. Rodney interpreted the question as Jan asking, "What problem do you have with me?" And as it turned out, this was the heart of the matter. He was aggravated by what he perceived to be his mother's lack of good character and how it was greatly impacting his life. He explained that his problems, and now his behavior, were the direct result of her bad character.

"I really value honesty in a person," he said.

Rather surprised at the insinuation, Jan replied, "And you think I don't?"

"No. You are dishonest."

"You really think so?"

"Yes, I do."

"Help me understand. Can you give me an example of when I have been dishonest with you or others?"

"Yesterday, you said we would go by the mall so I could buy those shoes we talked about. But you kept adding other errands to the trip, and we didn't go to the mall."

"Did you understand that your father called with an urgent matter that he needed me to take care of, and that it took precedent over a trip to the mall?"

"But you lied to me."

"Is that the only time you think I lied to you?"

"Of course not! You always lie about when we're going to leave the house to go places. You say we will leave in fifteen minutes, and it ends up being an hour. Or you will say we'll do something today, and it will be tomorrow. I can never depend on what you say!"

Boy, oh boy. Our son's standard for honesty was pretty high, but Jan needed to know he was serious and try to understand his perceived offense. Yes, he needed to make some adjustments too, but he was unable to see his own need for change until Jan demonstrated a willingness to improve her own character.

In this case, the issue was really one of communication, but you can see how his complaint was deeply rooted in a desire that his parents show themselves dependable. We did work it out eventually, but Jan and I both still struggle with deceiving ourselves about how much we can accomplish in a given amount of time. She knows that if I think I can complete a task in two hours, it's more likely to be five hours. Or if I think I'll be home from work by 6:00, it will be closer to 7:00. That said, if we invite you over for dinner, you can be certain we'll be ready if you show up on time—or at least that the food will be worth the wait!

I don't want to belabor this thought, but children are like mirrors; with rare exception, they reflect back the parents they see. If you don't like what you are seeing in your children, take a good look at yourself. If teens sense disrespect in you, they will be disrespectful. If they sense condescension in you, they will be condescending toward others. If they sense kindness in you, they are more likely to be kind to others.

You might find it interesting to talk with your teen about this point and ask if she believes it to be true. Describe what you see in her and ask if that's how she sees you. Ask about any weakness she sees in you and where you need to grow. Listen sincerely and then talk about the kind of character you want to live out. Ask her if she would be willing to grow with you in this area. Take notes during the discussion to show you are serious (if you are). It could be a very difficult conversation but also one of the most meaningful you'll ever experience with your teen.

My children are all adults now, and it remains a mystery to me how it works, but the character you develop is the character you pass on to your children. We're all familiar with phrases like "The apple doesn't fall far from the tree" and "He's a chip off the old block." As parents, we reproduce who we are, not what we wish our kids to be. If your produce is looking a bit moldy, inspect yourself.

Competence

The third bridge to building trust with your teen is competence. Are you good at what you do? Do you give your best effort to your work whether you're an employee or a volunteer? Do you make it a point to learn and grow in competence in the tasks that are required of you? Are you on a continuous improvement plan for your life? The fact that you're reading this book suggests that you are willing to improve. Are you better this year than last at handling your personal affairs and family communication?

Yes, we all have a lifelong weakness or two. Perhaps you simply don't have an aptitude for cooking, mechanical repairs, or bookkeeping. But are you increasingly competent in your areas of strength? And are you getting better at managing your relationships? Your continued growth matters to your children, and it's an integral part of building trust with your teen.

Consistency

The fourth bridge to building trust is consistency. Once a year is not enough for your children to feel your love or know that you're proud of them. It's not enough to usually be calm around your kids but then explode without warning when someone pushes the wrong button. It's not enough to occasionally ask them about the substance of their day. The daily habits of care, character, and communication are the building blocks of trust. We all know someone who is volatile and unpredictable. We never know if he or she will smile, crack a joke, or erupt with a hateful or physical response. So we tend to avoid that person whenever possible. It's crucial as a parent that you not be "that person."

Three Benefits of Losing Control of Your Kids

Even if you do everything right as a parent—you won't, but I'll humor you—as your children grow up, you're going to lose control of them. As I've said, this process is natural and normal. In fact, it is good and right. But losing control is a two-edged sword, and both sides of it will cut into your comfortable existence. Just when you feel like you have your feet under you as a parent, the ground shifts and everything changes.

The transfer of control from you to your growing child happens at an alarming pace during the teen years, and the continuous change will keep you off balance. But there are very real benefits to ceding control that you should not only welcome but embrace. Let's talk about three of these benefits.

Adult Conversation—A Benefit of Losing Control

We've already talked about this a bit. Adult conversation with your teen doesn't have to be a frightening prospect. In fact, it can be quite wonderful. And open communication is necessary if you're to have influence with your teen into adulthood. But to have the pleasure of adult conversations with your teen, you must continually build those bridges of trust, regardless of where things currently stand in your relationship.

Having adult conversations with your teen can rapidly deepen the quality of your interactions once the door of communication is cracked open. However, I suggest lowering your expectations for your initial conversations as this will help prevent you from becoming discouraged in the process. Your initial goal might be as simple as getting more than a one-word answer in response to a question. An important habit to learn as the parent of a teen is to ask an open-ended question and then allow a significant period of silence. Often, parents shoot themselves in the foot by violating one or both of these guidelines. If you ask questions that invite one-word answers, that is what you'll get. So asking "How was your day?" is not a good start—we all know the answer to that one.

If open and free conversation is not currently a habit with your teen, a great place for you to start is in the car. Naturally, your teen will have to remove his earbuds or headphones for you to start the process, but the shoulder-to-shoulder positioning offered by a car ride helps to reduce the sense of confrontation and interrogation that teens often feel when a parent tries to initiate conversation. I recently learned this "shoulder-to-shoulder" language from reading *Love and Respect* by Emerson Eggerichs. Dr. Eggerichs notes that men often prefer to relate to others shoulder-to-shoulder at work or in such activities as fishing, golfing, or driving. Women, on the other hand, tend to prefer face-to-face interaction in order to make a significant connection.[4]

Two parties in any relationship where there exists a low level of trust will be more comfortable engaging in conversation if they're not positioned face-to-face. Consider that in choosing when and where to start breaking the ice in a currently frozen relationship. That's why talking in the car (without headphones) can help you get started.

A friend of ours from Minnesota told us of a car conversation she had with her thirteen-year-old son one day after school. He had been diligently saving money to purchase some special bicycle shorts for wearing in bike races, and they had agreed that Margie would pick him up after school and drive him by the sporting goods store on the way home. As he got in the car, she initiated the conversation with some simple "How was your day?" questions. Then she asked, "Did anything different happen today?"

"Well, in health class we had a special sex-education presentation."

Carefully and with a bit of anxiety, Margie responded, "What did they talk about?"

"Oh, you know. You need to wear condoms for safe sex."

Margie felt she couldn't breathe as they both just stared out the windshield. For her, the silence was deafening. But she became even more distressed when her son broke the silence by saying, "I wonder if they will fit me..."

Now Margie's palms began to sweat, and her heart skipped a few beats. She kept her eyes forward as she gathered enough courage to calmly respond, "They say one size fits all."

"Mom!" her son cried out, "I'm talking about the bike shorts!"

Nervous laughter carried them the rest of the trip to the bike shop, where they could more comfortably talk about other things. But the memory of that shoulder-to-shoulder conversation would stay with them forever.

When you are side by side with one of your kids and you're gardening, cooking, fishing, building, or watching a ballgame together, it's the perfect time to explore their ideas and thoughts by asking questions that don't necessarily have a right answer. For example, "If you had a million dollars, what would you do with it?"

Hopefully, you're picking up on the key part you are to play in conversation with your teen: It's not about what *you* say to *her*; it's about getting *her* to talk to *you*. It's about getting her to open up about what she thinks of herself and the world around her. She has to tell you where she is in order for you to have a positive impact on her future. It's a lot like giving someone directions over the telephone. You first try to figure out where they are based on what they're seeing, hearing, and feeling. Once you've figured out where they are, only then do you have a real chance of guiding them to their destination.

Of course, the destination is not what life is all about. It's about making the journey together. All the great stories or movies we've enjoyed didn't thrill us because the heroes made it to the "Emerald City" but because they had an exciting journey to get there. So it is with our teens as we initiate the kinds of conversations that help them move further along their life's path.

Essential to knowing our teens is having conversations with them about issues that are important to them. Equally important is asking good questions to guide their thinking about those issues they're willing to talk about. Keep in mind that you're not trying to stump your teen. Instead, you want to ask questions that address areas he may have not considered. You will *not* build trust by lecturing to him or by clarifying your own opinions on the matter or by pronouncing "truth" to him. You build trust by listening to what *he* has to say.

So when do you, the parent, get to speak? You *are* speaking—just not with words. The important message you're sending is "I care about you" and "I am with you." There will be time for words, if you listen well; there will never be time for words if you don't. You've had at least twelve years to pour into your child, and there's probably no emergency need for information now. The need your teen has is to be understood and accepted. It takes a lot of courage for your teen to expose her inner self to you, and so you must be a safe place for her to reveal the turmoil of thoughts and values that's brewing beneath the crust of her behavior and attitudes. Though teens throw up walls of deception and barriers to knowing them, they really do want to be known. It's your job and privilege as a parent to know your child better than anyone else in this world, but you can only accomplish this by listening. If you will make yourself available to hear her process her inner thoughts without pointing out the errors in her thinking, she will eventually ask about your thoughts. And the door for you to speak will have swung open.

The teen years are discovery years in which your child is learning to make sense of all the facts and feelings he has gathered in life, to determine what is important and why. You will not help him discover this by saying again what you've already said or by saying it louder or more passionately. He will discover the answers he's seeking by talking through the issues with someone he trusts. Someone who will listen. Someone who will hear without reacting. Someone who will not be shocked that he could even *think* such things. Someone who will not shame him for questioning whether something is true or right. If you cannot be that kind of person for your teen, you will not know him because he will hide from you. The wall constructed between you will have been constructed out of either condemnation and shame and guilt, or out of indifference and inattentiveness and disbelief. If this wall already exists between you, you have to take it down brick by brick, or build a bridge over it with care, character, competence, and consistency.

One of the best role models I know for having conversations with kids lives in Indiana and has a ministry called Familyman. What a great name for the work Todd Wilson does, because he not only speaks and writes about fatherhood and family management. He lives it. And he lives it well, I might add. How do I know? I asked his children! Todd has a great reputation, but as I said earlier, a person's kids always know the real deal.

Todd asked one of his kids what kind of project he would like to do, and to his surprise, the kid said, "I would like to build a jet engine." *What?!?*

Todd didn't react outwardly but asked, "What do you know about jet engines?"

"Not much, but I'd like to make one."

"See what you can learn about it, and we will see about doing it."

Todd warns parents against killing the dreams of their kids and encourages them to fan the flames of thoughts and dreams that children express. Time and effort will sort out what is realistic. Some kids will surprise you with amazing results by pursuing their passions and interests.

Our youngest son had the idea that he wanted to build an electric go-cart that was street-legal. In other words, he wanted to build an electric car. Hudson was consumed with the efficiency and power of electric motors and batteries. It seemed to him a small step to assemble a car based on his "vast knowledge," and he shared his idea with two of his elderly great-uncles who were electrical engineers in their day. They listened to his ideas, then chuckled. One of them said, "Well, Hudson, it's not quite that easy. I don't think you can pull that off." To which he replied under his breath, and later said to me, "You'll see."

Hudson was not to be deterred from his dream. After high school, he went off to college to study electrical engineering. He became increasingly capable of understanding the complexities of energy, power, circuitry, switches, volts, and amperage. Little by little, the dream changed as he became more competent. He never built the electric car, but the dream of the electric car led him to a career as an electrical engineer. Day in and day out, he works with all the things he was learning for his dream car. Where would he be today if we had killed his wild dream when it seemed so possible to him?

Think back to your dreams as a teen. If you can recall some of the crazy ideas you had, you may find a bit of compassion welling up in your heart for your young dreamer. Instead of killing the dreams of your children, maybe you should ask, "What do you think it would take for that to happen?" Fan the flame of their ideas and dreams with questions, with resources, with tools and materials, and by putting them in touch with experts who can advise them. Childhood dreams sometimes die and sometimes change. But they should be given a chance to live and grow.

Adult conversations about dreams and goals can be serious fun, especially if you're willing to forget realism and let anything be possible. When that's the case, the conversation is really about what a person *wants* to happen—in other words, what the person *values*. When your teen talks to you about her values, you are really getting to know her inner person. Again, the key is listening. Keep in mind that once teens open up, they rarely use an economy of words. Instead, they ramble a bit while searching for just the right words to describe what they're envisioning. They may even stop and start over, trying again with different words. If you throw water on the fire of this word search, she might just give up and go find a better listener, one who may prove to be a terrible advisor.

Our teens have the ability to think for themselves, and they're going to do it. In fact, you *want* them to do it. No thinking parent wants a mindless child. Would you send your child off to college with instructions to accept without question everything he hears from everybody? Imagine telling your college-bound teen, "Don't ever think for yourself. Believe everything you hear in the classroom. And consume anything you're handed at a party." That's ludicrous!

Yet many of us are outraged if our teen dares to question something we've said, the way we do something, or heaven forbid, what we believe. You can't have it both ways. If you're not encouraging an inquiring mind, you're suppressing it.

Real Helpers—A Benefit of Losing Control

In a home with more than one child, getting help from your children begins quite early, often with the oldest child running to get a diaper for the baby. As time goes by, children want to help around the home more and more as they learn new skills and gain competence. But teens can take it to a whole new level that constitutes "real help." If they are encouraged to exercise control over their growing physical and mental abilities, their contribution to the family—and to their future—can be massive.

Technology. Members of the younger generation seem to have a natural affinity for handling technology. Smartphones, tablets, computers, and their software require very little explanation for those who have grown up in a world where tech is constantly advancing, always changing, so their minds are pliable and receptive to new things. Kids who grow up in a bilingual home have a similar capacity for speaking two languages interchangeably with hardly a noticeable shift in thinking.

When my oldest two children were in their mid-twenties, they spent two months bicycling across France, learning about vineyards, winemaking, and the French culture. Then they headed back across the Alps into Italy. On their journey, they found that the French and Italian locals living along the border were completely comfortable with both languages, easily moving back and forth from one to the other.

In a similar way, the digital universe makes perfect sense to teens who have never known a world without computers, and often they don't even recognize that tech-speak is a different language for the rest of us. Granted, many of you reading this book have grown up in the digital age and may not be able to relate to my difficulty with managing my passwords, much less accessing cloud storage or setting up a WordPress site. But your teens will no doubt do things far greater than you with the same tools you feel competent using.

Thus, our teens can be a tremendous help in navigating the digital world if we will but ask, and it will give them an opportunity to stretch themselves in an area of interest. If they don't immediately know the answers you seek, all the better—kids tend to be more interested in doing something they're not yet competent to do.

Teens are fully capable of learning bookkeeping programs, setting up automatic bill payments, and creating spreadsheets to track income and expenses. They can design Christmas cards and shower invitations, create video invitations, and put together memory montages of family events. Appealing to their interests and drawing upon their aptitude will put them in a sweet spot for new growth and development of useful skills.

Consider sending your teens to a business seminar, or enrolling them in a webinar to learn something your family should change about how you use your digital resources, and then let them try their hand at implementing it. I recommend sending teens to live events where they will meet other learners and have a chance to interact with an expert. These kinds of encounters help teens transition into thinking like an adult. You'll be surprised how much a live event can motivate teens to implement what they've learned. Chances are what your teen learns will help the household *and* improve your work and family processes.

Money. Often, the skills teen gain and put to use will result in a payday for them. I'm not talking about *your* money. I'm talking about other people paying them, which opens up a whole new area of benefit to the family. When teens begin earning their own money, they not only can buy some of their own stuff, but they can begin saving for things like education, clothes, activities, gifts for birthdays and Christmas—or the cost of their next training seminar! When money comes under your teen's control, it's a big opportunity for personal growth. Ideally, you will be there to come alongside your teen and ask good questions like "How much are you giving to charity?" and "How much do you plan to save?" and "What can you do with that money that will make it multiply?"

When teens learn how to handle money and understand that it won't "burn a hole in their pocket" if they save some of it, they can help the family in other ways. As they begin to recognize the value of a dollar, they may be able to help you stretch yours. Since their teen years, my kids have saved me untold amounts of money by finding us deals on everything from mobile phone plans to sporting equipment. Okay, I might be using the word "save" loosely. What they usually did was help me buy more stuff for the same amount of money. I guess that's a kind of saving. I know it's what my wife means by it.

Making money and finding deals are great ways teens can help, but they can also help by understanding the family budget, especially if money is often tight. For many of us, it takes everything we make and then some just to get by every month. Teens who understand this can be much more compassionate about what the family is able to do for fun and entertainment. They're usually mature enough to appreciate specifically how much money comes in each month and see it on a budget sheet along with what you pay in rent or mortgage, utilities, food, and other expenses. Giving your teen real knowledge of the family's financial position demonstrates real respect. If you handle the discussion seriously and explain the budget to them as you would to another adult, your teen will probably respond maturely. Most teens appreciate having a real adult conversation about real-world things like family finances.

Now, I'm not recommending parents sit their teens down with a copy of the budget every time they ask for something a little pricey and rub their nose in the fact that there's no money for it. That's not a conversation. Resist the temptation to go there when you're stressed, because there are no winners in this type of exchange. If you can remain calm and lay out the facts without a lot of emotion, then you should feel comfortable inviting your teen into the discussion about family finances.

If you're blessed to have room in your family budget for extra things, your discussions may be less about where you're going to find the money and more about setting priorities. Talk with your teen about how much is reasonable to spend on a particular item and whether it's a required purchase or an "extra."

Train your teen to understand that having money is not about your social status or the pleasures money can afford. Teach your teen that money in our hands is simply a tool for accomplishing something good, and we have to determine wisely how to put it to use. Whatever your financial situation, your teen must begin to understand how money works and why it makes a great servant but a terrible master.

Transportation. A major area in which teens are capable of helping involves family transportation. Unless you live in Manhattan or downtown Chicago, having a teen who can drive can be a game changer. Instantly, your errand list is reduced by 40 percent if you're willing to extend shifting control to use of the family car. Teens can do grocery shopping, pick up laundry, or even just drive themselves to events, lessons, or ball practice. Naturally, a degree of competence must be achieved to drive a car, particularly in city traffic, but that can only be gained through experience.

When your family can afford the increase in insurance premiums to make it possible, getting your teen a driver's permit is highly recommended. Even so, many families make the mistake of limiting their teens' opportunities to get behind the wheel. It's as though they think that just keeping a permit in his pocket for a year will make their teen a qualified, capable driver. Whenever possible, your new permit holder should be driving, with you at his side. Rain or shine, night or day, traffic or no, a teen needs supervised experience with his trusted guide calmly teaching him to think like a seasoned driver:

"You're going to need to turn right about a mile ahead. When would you like to get in the proper lane for that?"

"Up ahead, traffic is merging in from the right, so don't be surprised by it."

"If it starts raining, how much extra distance will you want to allow between you and the car in front of you?"

There is no doubt the risk is rising, and it can be frightening to sit in the passenger seat when your child is behind the wheel. But this doesn't change the fact that your teen needs to learn to drive, and you are the one to teach her. She can attend driver education classes, but let's face it: She's going to need more than a few hours' experience to become a competent driver. Teaching your teen to drive will open worlds of opportunity for her, and you'll also be giving yourself a break.

Organizations like AAA and the National Highway Safety Administration provide very good course materials online to guide you in effectively coaching your developing driver. Grandparents can also be an excellent resource. They want more time with their grandchildren, even if it means taking them for a drive to log the hours teens need to achieve competence.

Emotional Maturity—A Benefit of Losing Control

Emotional maturity? In teens? Right about now, you may be wondering if I even understand the definition of emotional maturity. I wonder this myself as I write it. But bear with me a moment as I explain.

During the post-pubertal years, the brain is bathed with hormones and neurotransmitters that enable it to do things that have previously been very difficult. For example, logical reasoning—the process of recalling stored information, comparing it to other stored information or to something new, then assessing its value—is a new and valuable skill. Or at least it's a greatly expanded skill for teens that allows them to choose to value an emotion or ignore it by replacing it with reasons why something is better or worse. I'm not saying that teens are proficient at setting aside emotion to reach a logical conclusion, but they do have the growing capacity for such a thing.

Recently, our four-year-old granddaughter Cora came to visit GranJan's house for a few days without her siblings. Fun times were had involving such activities as painting, swimming, cooking, reading books, and swinging. The day before Cora's parents were to pick her up, her mother made a video call to touch base with her, and Cora talked excitedly for several minutes about everything she had done.

Suddenly, little Cora was overcome with emotion.

She wanted her mother to see her, to see how beautiful her new dress was and how wonderful her coloring pages were. She burst into tears because her mother couldn't hold her right then and tell her how proud she was. No amount of reasoning, no amount of explaining that it was just one more day until she got her wish would comfort her. Cora's emotions had free rein, and she just had to cry it out.

A teen, on the other hand, may experience the same surge of desire and emotional need but can usually buffer it by reasoning that Mom's video commendation is as good as a hug, that tomorrow is but a short delay, or that as accomplishments go, a coloring page is rather a small thing and not really worthy of all the fuss. Or if she's in public, she may reason, *If I put on an emotional show here, that young man over there may take compassion on me and produce another response I will like just as well.* While both good and bad uses of logic may appear on the scene, all this juggling of options is actually a complex task that might be called "maturity."

My four-year-old granddaughter did not have the ability to suppress her emotion, even if she had the ability to suppress the crying. The emotion had to run its course, and she was at its mercy. A teenager, however, has the ability to either control her emotion or let emotion control her, because now her brain can process multiple options at the same time and choose to assign greater value to one thing or the other, thus taking control. She is now able to win many of the inner battles that just a couple of years earlier would have resulted in her melting down or freezing up.

Teens have the option of either inviting the emotions in or telling them to leave. Granted, teens still frequently operate in the emotional, excitable realm, but it is by choice or habit, not because they can't process things differently.

Emotional maturity, then, is the ability to either grant or deny control to one's emotional response, whether it be happy, sad, joyful, or angry.

As a practicing physician, I experience a lot of frustration with a medical community and society where it's commonplace to assign a label to any expression that someone doesn't like, such as depression, anxiety, ADD, or defiance disorder. A diagnosis is quickly rendered and a one-size-fits-all treatment plan involving pills and potions appears to make all things smooth again.

The biggest need I see in such situations is for a trusted advisor to help teens take control of their emotional response to stressors. We need to train them to use logical deduction to formulate a considered response to whatever problem life throws their way. Many of the young adults I see for anxiety and depression need coaching and counsel far more than they need medicine. Parents can help their teens exercise and develop their new ability to balance emotion with logic, which is a process that leads to self-control. When parents become overly focused on the teen's emotional response, they're training the teen to let her emotions control her, much like four-year-old Cora.

As parents, it is our responsibility to help our teens learn to use their new capacity for self-control. Without oversimplifying, let me say that emotions *can* be controlled. But don't confuse self-control with the suppression of emotion, where a person is numb or feels nothing at all. Emotional suppression, as discussed in the book *How We Love* by Milan and Kay Yerkovich, is usually rooted in some emotional trauma or some deep, unmet emotional need that makes the individual afraid to allow the emotion to come to the surface.[5] The feeling it carries is tied to a memory the individual has buried deep in his or her subconscious as a survival mechanism. This is not what I'm referring to when I talk about emotional self-control.

With increasing maturity, most of us have the ability to manage the effect our emotions have on us. Fear, excitement, rage, enthusiasm, disappointment, hatred—all of these are associated with thoughts, and thoughts can be managed, evaluated, and expressed or rejected. With a little training, teens have the ability to do this. That is emotional maturity, and it's a real benefit to both teens and their parents.

Now we turn our attention to finding opportunities to transfer more control into the capable hands of our teens.

CHAPTER 11

Trading Control for Influence with Your Teen

Remember, our mission as parents is to eliminate our children's need for us. When we have finished our task, they will be fully capable of carrying on without us ordering their day or telling them how to think. To this day, I would like to discuss some things with my father, but his absence in no way hinders my continued growth and productivity. Your child will need to be able to function without you very soon, and that means he needs you to hand over more control, with an ever-decreasing amount of input.

In the same way they learn to drive, teens learn to manage some important aspects of life as you first are by their side, then watching from a distance, then occasionally checking in, and finally, completely forgetting about it until they come to you and ask for help with a problem. Some of the areas of life we'll discuss in this chapter include time management, relationships, social media, life direction, and professional development. But keep in mind that the principles we discuss in these five areas can be applied in other situations.

Time Management

The lives of our teens tend to be very busy; almost every minute of their days is scheduled for some activity. As I listen to families tell me about their schedules, a wave of dizziness comes over me. I often think, *Were our kids hyper-scheduled like that? Did our kids have time to think and dream, or were we scheduling their every breath?* (It's easy to forget some of the details because the years went by so fast. As the saying goes, the days are long, but the years are short.)

Today's families need a personal assistant to keep track of all their commitments! Thankfully, most of us already have one on that mini-computer we call a smartphone, which provides a way to share calendars so that everyone in the family can see where everyone should be at a given moment. Such tools are helpful to remind us of the details of life. It is precisely this point I want to make here.

As children mature, they must be trained to look not just at what's next on the schedule, but also what's coming up in the next week and the next month. They need to be taught to pace themselves, to plan out the time they will need to finish a project or study for a test. They can also be trained to plan fun events, even learning to be proactive about recreation.

Most college freshmen who drop out of school don't leave because they're not smart enough or because they run out of money. They drop out, or are kicked out, because they couldn't manage their time. Classes and assignments were missed because they could not, or would not, look at their deadlines and realize there wasn't time to go to a movie or attend a party. There wasn't time to play video games late into the night and still get enough sleep to be up and ready for an early class. I have heard numerous accounts from college administrators about the effects of an undisciplined life. Parents often played a role in a students' unpreparedness by overlooking opportunities to shift control to their teens while they were still at home.

Of course, it's not enough to turn over control to our teens and just let them fail. Shifting control involves a training process of walking our teens through their calendar, helping them plan the coming days and weeks, and teaching them that failing to plan is the same as planning to fail. It is a tremendous boost to teens for parents to be engaged enough to first see that they have made a plan to accommodate their scheduled events, and then to watch to see if they live out the plan they have made. Remember, the greatest influence is in not in trying to catch them doing something wrong but in trying to catch them doing something right and praising them for it. In this way, you can help your teen become everything he or she wants to be.

As in *The One Minute Manager*, where the "best manager in the world" would check in with an employee frequently after he had taken on a new responsibility, and less often as he saw the employee being successful, parents need to check in on their child's plan frequently in the early stages to help her learn to schedule effectively. Efficient use of a schedule will help her win in life.

A bit of gentle accountability helps, so at the end of the day each item on her to-do list is checked off or reassigned to another spot on the calendar. When teens are lax about managing their time, or not effectively using their planning tools, the temptation arises for the parent to become heavy-handed and intervene in the process. However, we must resist the urge to save our teens from their oversight and allow them to get into a pickle every now and then. This is a natural consequence that helps reinforce the need for working the plan.

Electronic calendars work great for some, yet others prefer the old-school approach of a paper calendar or organizer. Only a few, like my wife, can keep all the details straight in her head. There is no one perfect method, but for training purposes, a schedule needs to be viewable by more than one person, so the mental calendar is not an option during the training period. Keep in mind that the purpose of this tool is to lead your teen to the point where he is in complete control of his time; it's not a method for taking back some of the control from him.

Dating and Relationships

Surrendering control in the area of relationships can be a scary proposition. We're all wary of the out-of-control, passionate teen relationships often portrayed in movies. And I'm not advocating for no parental oversight in relationships. I'm suggesting you transfer control to your teen as he or she demonstrates self-control and discernment when it comes to interpersonal relationships.

No parents want their child to experience emotional trauma as the result of a friendship or romantic relationship. We have an innate desire to protect our children from those things that have wounded us in the past, thus our painful memories can drive us to be overprotective.

Our desire is that our teens will develop the understanding, skills, and confidence to communicate freely and genuinely with all people, whether male or female, superiors or subordinates (at work), acquaintances or strangers. We want them to be able to read other people and perceive whether they're sincere or have a hidden agenda. Ideally, speaking and listening would involve a natural flow of thoughts and ideas that allow our teens to really know others while making themselves known. We want them to be able to set aside their own interests and desires to attend to the interests and needs of others. We also want them to develop the kind of character that draws others to them, even as they remain unimpressed with themselves. In short, we want our teens to embrace life.

Sounds like a wonderful place, almost unbelievable. How do our teens get to this place? I want you to know that it is possible! I've seen it hundreds of times as, with care and wisdom, parents applied the principles of transferring control to their teens in the area of relationships.

Transferring control in this area is frightening for both parties. Parents, we all remember the excitement and nervousness that accompanied our first date or the first time we were allowed to go somewhere with a special friend. On the other side of the door, dads across the ages have feared the knock announcing the arrival of a boy who's interested in their daughter.

How can we, as parents, strike the right balance as our teen's protector and guide? It will be less by *perspiration*, more by *inspiration*. Everyone needs someone to inspire them. We need cheerleaders around us and heroes ahead to encourage us to fight through the uncomfortable and fearful things of life. We are not empowered when someone clears the path of obstacles to make it easy for us. But we can be inspired to overcome hurdles when someone shouts, "I know you can do it! Don't give up! You're almost there!"

In the 2006 movie *Facing the Giants*, a football player is given the seemingly impossible task of crawling thirty yards on his hands and feet while carrying a team member on his back. Blindfolded, he crawls while his coach cheers him on, telling him, "You can do it! You're almost there! Don't give up! I know you've got it in you!" Upon declaring him finished, the coach removes the blindfold to reveal to the young man that he has traveled not thirty yards but a *hundred* yards! With a little inspiration, that player learned he was able to do far more than he believed possible. And he inspired his teammates who watched him accomplish the feat.

We must inspire our teens with a vision of what it looks like to treat a date with honor and respect, how to make someone feel special and safe in their presence, how to live and speak with honesty, and how to handle their emotions with integrity. These may be noble attributes to describe a teen relationship, but one way or another, you need to instruct your teen in what an adult relationship should be like. In reality, you have been teaching him for the past decade—by how you treat your spouse and your in-laws, how you speak of your boss and neighbors, and how you drive in traffic. The way you live will speak louder than your words, but words are also important. Tell him stories of how you navigated romance to find your spouse, even if your choices were not always exemplary. Tell him how you want him to be spared the consequences you had to deal with and inspire him to imagine it better for himself.

This needs to start before your teen walks out the front door for his first date. Hopefully, you begin this process years before so it can begin to affect his deep thoughts—not just his thoughts of how to be charming enough to get the girl but also thoughts of how he should strive to be worthy of the girl. Resources are abundant to help you discuss the ways guys and girls are wired to think differently and desire different things from a relationship. Find one to help you open discussion with your teen about the opposite gender. Teens can find these talks quite revealing and often realize their attempts to impress are totally missing the mark.

They need to know basic concepts of polite conversation, such as talking to others about *them*, not about yourself. They should be comfortable with speaking to authorities with respect and honor, and how to honor your companion when moving through a crowd or walking down the street. Knowing what constitutes appropriate touch can give your teen both freedom and restraint. Watch for opportunities to point out good examples of these things in movies or stories your read together. Although movies are notorious for depicting relationships that are highly sexualized, you will find abundant useful examples of a couple walking into a party together, getting into a car, introducing the other person to a friend, or giving preference to their date.

Pushing your teen into a one-on-one dating scenario before she's ready is not recommended. Instead, look for opportunities for her to practice shorter times of interaction with someone she likes, such as a thirty-minute outing for ice cream or a bike ride in the neighborhood. Short, low-risk encounters with minimal expectations on both parts give teens the chance to experiment with their freedom without much chance of major failure. Helping our teens experience safe encounters may take some time and planning, but such outings are important opportunities for them to recognize their weaknesses and see the need for growth.

When my youngest son graduated from high school, a friend gave him a book titled *How to Be a Gentleman*. It was a beautiful little black book that went unread and somehow found its way to my study, where it caught my eye one day. After fifty years of living and learning, I soon discovered there were plenty of things I didn't know about being a gentleman. Some of the pointers I found curious, such as "A gentleman should never wear a tuxedo before 5:00 in the afternoon." But I also found that the book offered great advice on topics like how to introduce yourself and your guest in a variety of settings, how to write a thank-you note, how to respond to an invitation, how to move with a lady through a crowd, and how to appropriately send flowers. A young man in pursuit of a lady must first learn these kinds of skills and then put them into practice.

Communication Skills and Leadership

Relationships all around us—not just the romantic ones—are important and worthy of your teen's attention. All individuals are due respect, but learning to communicate well with others helps teens to grow confident in the freedom and control they have been given.

Our oldest child, Caleb, was involved with the 4-H youth organization and had experienced a degree of success in public speaking competitions, which led to his appointment to serve on some statewide committees at the age of fourteen. The committees were a mixture of teens and adult professionals, and they were making organizational decisions or finding funding for different programs 4-H offered. As a committee member, our son was expected to help raise funds from community contacts. We sat down with Caleb to begin making a list of people he should contact about making donations. My wife doesn't have a shy bone in her body, and she was rapidly dictating a list of doctors, lawyers, leaders of the chamber of commerce, business owners, and bank presidents. We gathered the phone numbers and helped him develop a script, then watched him sit nervously at the kitchen table, staring at the list before him.

"When are you going to start calling them, Caleb?" Jan asked.

"In a minute."

But several minutes passed, and still he was frozen. So Jan picked up the phone, dialed the first number, and put the receiver in his hand. Before he could bolt, a polite voice came through the phone: "Progressive Bank. Thanks for calling. How may I help you?"

He quickly looked down at his script. "Hi, this is Caleb Smith. I was calling for Mr. Cummings. Is he available to speak with me?" Before he could get more nervous, the phone clicked over to the bank president, and Caleb continued following his script. Much to his surprise, talking with a bank president was not so hard, and before long he was speaking freely with the professionals on his list, referring to his script when he got stuck or nervous.

Teens need similar training in everyday situations that are not assigned to them by some organization or forced upon them by their parents. For example, at the supermarket, they may need to appeal to the produce manager for additional stock to fill their grocery list, or inform the store manager that they have broken an item. They may need to speak to a restaurant manager to request a refund for an undercooked meal or to commend a waitperson on an excellent job. There are appropriate ways to confront and effective ways to commend. There are winsome ways to appeal for help and gracious ways to offer assistance; meaningful ways to encourage and memorable ways to comfort. Useful words, phrases, questions, and answers require practice to make them a comfortable part of a teen's vocabulary. You can help by creating situations for practice so that your teen can grow in his ability to connect with others.

As teens mature, they will need to play several different roles at the same time, and parents need to train them to identify and understand how to communicate in these situations. At the same time they're speaking as a customer to the store manager, they may also be acting as an authority caring for a younger sibling or as a peer greeting a friend who passes by. These various roles are colliding, forcing the teen to rapidly shift from one to the other, giving the appropriate attention to each listener. Sounds a lot like what parents do, doesn't it? It sounds this way because your teen is becoming you, while outgrowing his or her need for you.

Embedded in these different relationships is the concept of leading and following. Until the teen years, opportunities for our children to lead others outside the family are usually minimal, but they should have been learning to lead themselves by using logic, delaying gratification, waiting their turn patiently, thinking of others' needs before their own, and stepping outside their comfort zone in service to others. Leadership is a learned skill. Some teens have more natural leadership ability than others, but all have the capacity to learn and grow in this area. Leadership skills help move our teens to a place where they can use the control they've been given to benefit someone beside themselves. They must learn that leadership is not about the leader but, rather, about serving the mission and the people involved.

Almost every youth organization I know is focused on leadership development. That should tell you something about its importance at this time in a young person's life. We, as parents, must capitalize on the energy and momentum that naturally accompany this age to place our teens in situations where they can develop and practice leadership skills—situations that require slightly more skills than they already have, thus stimulating their growth. It's wonderful when the inspiration to grow outside of their comfort zone comes from someone besides their parents, thereby eliminating the friction of them blaming us for getting them into something too hard. I've had fun being able to say, "Don't look at me. I had nothing to do with it. But you need to figure out how you're going to take care of it."

One day, our son Rodney, the skateboarder, got so made at Jan because he thought she had encouraged a youth leader at one of the area churches to ask Rodney to lead a Bible study group for young skaters at the skatepark. Jan had nothing to do with it. In fact, she was as surprised as he that someone had asked a sixteen-year-old boy to lead a discussion group. Yet Jan thought he was capable of influencing the younger skaters, but Rodney was not excited about the responsibility.

Of course, Rodney had already started a construction company to build the skate park at that church, and he had impressed the younger skaters with both his knowledge of skate park construction and his ability to ride all the ramps and rails on his skateboard. The youth pastor likewise had grown to respect Rodney through the whole construction process and subsequent events. As the youth pastor watched his interaction with the younger skaters, he recognized that Rodney had influence with the boys, so he asked Rodney to lead the group.

As parents, we stepped back from the scene to watch our young man rise to the challenge. He learned to plan a lesson and lead a discussion of it. The seriousness with which he took on the responsibility was matched by the seriousness in the response of his mother when he complained to her that she should not have pushed him into leading the group. "Rodney, you are talking to the wrong person. You're going to take that up with your heavenly Father, because He orchestrated it that you should do this thing, not me." And with that, the issue was closed. Rodney was the leader, the influencer on skate days.

Your child in different ways will be faced with opportunities to assume control and lead others. I implore you to be ready to encourage her toward becoming a responsible leader. Find her resources and training in leadership, utilizing some of the many programs offered by schools and communities that want to help develop your young leader. Equipping her to lead is like giving her wings to fly.

Learning healthy leadership will help our teens in school, business, volunteerism, and even in love. Yes, leadership is healthy for one's love life. It's all about communication, having a proper view of oneself and others, and living out the kind of character that is not self-focused.

As teens grow in control of their own will and their own fears, it can be exciting for parents to loosen the reins and let them soar. Once we stop struggling to hold on to control, we can take part in helping them to grow toward complete independence.

Helping Your Teen to Navigate Social Media

The world of communication has undergone tectonic shifts over the last two decades, and older generations are working hard to understand the use of new tools that disseminate news and personal information at dizzying speeds that teens see as normal. No longer does word travel "through the grapevine" but is instantly sent with audible alerts of its arrival to your phone or watch so that everyone in the vicinity is curious to know what's being said. Not only words but also photos and videos that could exalt or debase a person are instantly shared with hundreds, thousands, or even millions, with no way for their subject to intervene or save face. Elsewhere, live feeds of practical jokes unleash tidal waves of embarrassment and shame on their victims.

Gossips have never had to verify their facts before sharing with the next person, but now gossip is playing in a league of its own. Anyone can say anything on a social media platform anonymously without the sender feeling the need to talk it through with a trusted friend ahead of time. Before you can say, "Don't look, Ethel!" it's already posted on Instagram, Snapchat, TikTok, Facebook, and YouTube, going out to everyone in your social circle.

Meanwhile, teens suffer in silence as they watch themselves become the butt of a joke or the center of a controversy. A helpful tally of likes and retweets quantifies their shame as all the world is informed of their real or imagined flaws, producing in them the certainty that life is not worth living. Never again can they step into a classroom and face the people they thought were their friends but who have shown, loud and clear, that they value the laughter their hurtful comments received more than they care about the pain and anguish they've caused. This is the ugly face of cyberbullying. In this world, it's every teen for himself or herself. This is the opposite of community.

Maybe I exaggerate. Maybe it's not "every teen for herself." But for the one suffering, it may as well be. And for the insecure teen who has not yet been the butt of the joke, she finds it safer to jump onto the dogpile than to try to defend the victim. Maybe by adding a clever remark to the string of insults, someone will notice her and "like" her. The false hierarchy created by social media is a brutal force, and the only antidote is a healthy dose of self-control and respect for others.

When my mother died in 2014, my siblings and I went through her keepsakes and found her scrapbook from high school, dating back to 1946. We were shocked to find in it a letter addressed to her from her classmates. She was the senior class president, and they were threatening her with a recall vote if she did not change her ways. The letter did not specify the infraction, nor did her typed-out response, which she had saved on the adjacent page. I was so curious about my mother's gross sin that I tracked down several of the people who signed the letter. To my dismay, none could remember ever sending the letter, much less what the issue was. But what resulted from their letter of confrontation was a desirable change in my mother triggered by actions of a community concerned enough about character that they confronted her directly, appealing to her integrity.

My mother wrote in response:

> Dear members of the warning committee,
>
> I do dearly thank you for your note. You may think this is a revengeful note, but I do mean it. I must say that my behavior today was not the way the president of a class is expected to act. I want to apologize to the whole class for my behavior. I know I shouldn't have acted the way I did today, but I just couldn't help it.

I'm writing this note because I know that you are my real friends, for only a true friend would tell me my mistakes so I could correct them before it did cause me embarrassment.

In conclusion I will say that I hope you will not have to send me a sweet little note like this again. Thanks ever so much for sending the "Warning."

Social media in 1946 took the shape of a typewriter and hand-delivered notes addressing perceived wrongs with appeals to "change your ways." The note was an attempt to spare my mother embarrassment, unlike today's social media that seems hellbent on causing embarrassment and shame. It truly is a different world our teens face.

Yielding control to your teen in the area of social media is terrifying but necessary. It is the new telephone and email and is ever expanding its capabilities and nuances. Communication in the business world of the present and the future appears to be headed for immersion in social media, so we must learn to help our preteens and teens use these tools effectively, efficiently, and respectfully. True character can be communicated through social media, as can care, competence, and consistency. (Do you recognize these words from the previous chapter?)

I don't know if my mother was coached in her response to the warning committee back in 1946, but I know she had been taught to speak respectfully to others, and her training came through loud and clear in her response. Your teens need guidance in how to respond to others with grace, respect, honesty, and wisdom. Social media posts as a means of communication are tricky and sometimes treacherous, but our kids can and must grow in this area. You and I can also grow as we help them navigate the turbulence.

However, training our children to respond to others with grace and truth should not be confined to the online world. Hopefully, you have been working with your child from a very early age to consider how the listener will hear and respond to their words. We first train our kids to communicate with physical gestures, then words, and then the subtle nuances of tone and inflection. With digital communication, however, all the rules change, because no longer are there clues of body language, tone of voice, or social context to give meaning to our words. Our words fly naked and alone into the ether, and others interpret our meaning and motive through the lens of their own emotions and past experience, of which we know nothing.

I urge you to seek out and take advantage of resources that provide parents with tools for training kids to carefully and wisely use this powerful platform. Keep in mind that all social media are by design addictive. It's so easy to scroll to the next post and then next and then "just one more." It's hard to stop, close the app, and move on to something else. And then there is the addictive nature of "likes," which affect the brain much like chemical substances. Likes symbolize a gain in reputation, causing users to constantly compare themselves to their peers.

We need to equip our teens with strategies to keep social media from consuming their minutes and hours or being the constant focus of their thoughts. Helping our teens discipline themselves to resist the pull of social media is a way of guiding them to use the control we have ceded to them. Encouraging them to maintain a "tech-free zone" is an idea that has worked for many families. Some families go so far as to keep a basket designated as the drop spot for phones during mealtimes and joint activities. This can also help parents curb distractions by putting their own phones in the basket. It's also a good idea to declare meals at restaurants to be technology-free so you can actually connect with one another, unlike so many who spend the meal staring at their phones.

Also, developing a planned time for rest from technology is important for a teen's health, especially during hours scheduled for sleep. Medical studies have shown that the type of light emitted from phone screens disrupts the circadian rhythm of sleep and waking. This light has an effect on the brain similar to sunlight that indicates to the brain that it's time to awaken. Yet many people complain of having difficulty falling to sleep and then resort to viewing social media or television, both of which stimulate the brain. This effect is sustained for a period of time, meaning sleep cycles can take days to adjust after any withdrawal from media.

I recommend both parents and teens set a bedtime for their screens as well as for their bodies. Newer phones have a bedtime setting that will help users establish and maintain this habit. Training your teen to declare some freedom from the instant communication culture can prevent future addiction to technology. It's difficult to ignore those little chirps signaling that you have a message or new post, but it's a sign of growing self-control when you can. Conversations with your teens about appropriate times and places to ignore the notifications can help them set boundaries for themselves.

I work in the medical clinic on weekdays, and often when I am talking to a patient, my phone will ding to indicate that I have received a message. My patients are paying good money to talk to me, and they expect me to give them my attention. So when the phone demands my attention, I have a decision to make: Do I prioritize the phone or the patient? Painting a scenario like this for teens can help them define times or situations they may encounter when they should practice ignoring the phone.

Patients often see me ignore the sound and continue our discussion, but there are times when I slip the phone from my pocket, look at the screen for a second, then drop it back out of sight and continue the discussion without missing a beat. Maybe I've been expecting an important call or response to a question. Otherwise, my intention is to let the patient know I heard it, understand what it is, and most importantly, that at that moment he or she is more important than others who are trying to reach me. The way we manage phone intrusions communicates to others how we value *them* and *their* time. So evaluate your own habits and help your teen objectively evaluate himself. Ask questions to guide his thoughts on the matter. Two helpful resources I have found are *Screens and Teens* by Dr. Kathy Koch[1] and *Taming the Techno-Beast* by Todd Wilson.[2] Seek to influence your teens to make good choices, but try to avoid exerting control unless things are dangerously out of control. Self-control is the goal, not parent-control.

Driving the Family Car

The ability to drive is a necessary skill in most parts of our country, yet many regions have such high-volume traffic that it's a real challenge to teach a beginner the basics and advance them to a level of competence. Driving in urban areas comes with risks, as well as the expense of insuring a teen driver. Yet the fact remains that the ability to drive can open doors of opportunity for your child, and it is worth the effort to find ways for him or her to become competent. Many valuable activities for teens involve places and schedules not accessible via public transportation and are immensely inconvenient for those who must drive them.

I mentioned earlier that grandparents are often an option to help train beginning drivers. Years ago, we visited an elderly aunt and uncle when our two oldest were teens. We let the oldest child drive on much of the trip across country. Our relatives wanted to take us to an apple orchard for a picnic, and they asked our second-oldest child drive them in their nice car on curvy country roads to the remote location. It was a treat for our daughter to drive two people who were so calm and encouraging. To this day, she loves narrow country roads and the memory of her time with those relatives.

Besides learning the skill of driving, there is the care and management of the car, whether it is the vehicle the rest of the family uses or one designated for use by the teen. We chose the option of getting a used car for our children's use, and it got "passed down" to younger children as their turn came along. But I would probably do it differently today after reading a few books and hearing from friends about their experiences in this regard. For one thing, I made the decisions regarding the vehicle's selection, purchase, maintenance, and usage, thus missing a tremendous opportunity to train my kids in some decisions and habits they needed to learn on their own. In the end, they survived and are doing well. But it would have been better for them if I had ceded more of the control over the car.

If you are uncertain of the approach you want to take and are open to other ideas, I recommend reading chapter 6 of *The Money Smart Family* by Steve and Annette Economides, which covers key things to consider when deciding how to manage automobile use, insurance, and other related concerns.[3] The Economides have made a lifelong study of financial efficiency and ways to train your children in the wise use of money. At the end of the book you're now reading, you will find an excellent model for establishing a "community car" to be shared by all the driver-eligible children in a family. This method was effectively used by a close friend, though I discovered it too late to implement it with my own kids.

Regardless of how you manage cars and driving, it's important that you have a plan to help your teen develop these skills. How do teens become safe drivers? Experience! So have yours drive you everywhere when they are learning. Yes, they should begin in parking lots and neighborhood streets, but they must eventually learn to deal with traffic, freeways, and bad weather. They must drive to learn how to drive safely in any situation, and you are there to guide their thinking, awareness, and decisions. But keep the end in mind—you are prepping them to be safe without your always being in the passenger seat.

Driving schools are available in some areas to teach driver performance, not just driver safety. They often set up automobile-control issues for students to practice managing, such as slippery conditions, obstacles in the road, high-speed maneuvers, and even flats or blowouts. I've read testimonies of father-daughter teams who attended such schools and had a blast together learning to drive while making memories and having fun along the way.

Conversation with Adults

Is the whole world age-segregated? No, it is not! In fact, we do our children a great disservice if we limit them to groupings of their age peers throughout their childhood and young adult years. I can think of no situation where adults are expected to socialize with only their peers based on age grouping outside of a nursing home.

Being socially adept with people from other age and culture groups is a hugely important skill for children to learn. Yet we're always trying to group children with other children, teens with other teens, single people with other single people, and so on. I would appeal to you to think larger for the sake of your children and yourself, as well as for our communities and country.

Our lives are enriched by encountering others different from ourselves. Without this kind of interaction, we are not stimulated to grow in our skills, abilities, and understanding. A saying I love goes like this: "You will be the same person in five years as you are today, except for the people you meet and the books you read." I have found this to be mostly true. Each of us needs to step out of his or her comfort zone now and then to experience other people and ideas. But to experience other people, conversation is necessary.

How often have you asked yourself, "What do I say to them?" Most of us ask that question internally anytime we meet someone new, but teens ask it with a feeling of terror—unless they have already developed the tools of conversation and gained some experience using them. To do so, however, requires going through some uncomfortable times of "practice."

Practicing conversational skills should really begin in a children's early years with simple things like ordering their own meal at a restaurant or purchasing tickets at the movie theater. But having mature conversations with an adult is the destination, and that can happen at most any age with the proper training. Learning a variety of starter questions is a great beginning, but the driving force behind effective conversation is learning to be interested in other people.

Many years ago, when we were studying World War II as a family, Jan had an idea to help the kids better understand the history in context by interviewing some veterans of the war. We knew several individuals in the community who had witnessed the war firsthand, and we scheduled visits with them. As I recall, we prepared some questions for the children to ask after we were all introduced and sat down. Those encounters became a model for our children to open a conversation and show interest in others. The kids did more than gather information; more importantly, they learned about reaching out to others and establishing relationships.

Through those interviews, the children became able and interested in interacting with adult men and women who gave them respect in return and helped them to grow into adulthood. Some of those "old men" would later introduce my kids to influential researchers, educators, businesspeople, and even representatives to the U.S. Congress. It all began with learning to talk with and take interest in someone in a different age group. People who are different from us change us and help us grow.

How can we train our teens to interact with adults and different segments of society? Among the first things they need to learn is how to make eye contact in a pleasant way to indicate their openness to connect. This demonstrates that they place value on the other person. An appropriate greeting may be a handshake, a nod of the head, a smile, a word, or a touch. All of these require some training, especially if cultural differences are involved. Even if cultural customs are crossed, a sincere attempt to connect is usually appreciated, allowing teens to build bridges outside their peer group. This is critical to their future success in this world because most opportunities they pursue after high school— for example, jobs, admittance to a college or technical school, renting an apartment—will likely require them to negotiate with someone who is not their own age. They must know how to communicate with experienced adults at an adult level.

Throughout my school years, I struggled to connect well with others. Few of my peers ever suspected it because I forced myself to interact with them until I developed enough confidence to overcome my fears. But as my peer group broadened in my early career, I quickly realized I needed more tools to help me successfully interact with those who were more established and respected than myself.

An ad I found in an airline magazine proposed just the solution. A program called "How to Talk to Anyone About Anything" by Leil Lowndes was being touted as a miracle tool for communication. I immediately ordered the recordings of her teaching, and all the Smiths listened to them together. With confidence, I can say we acquired many tools to help us communicate with others in a wide variety of settings. A side benefit was its positive effect on interaction in our home. Today, my adult children still refer to and use many of the concepts they first learned from those recordings, concepts that have helped them navigate the business world successfully.

Learning to maneuver in the world of adults can be done with little risk when no one expects you to be there. An example of this is professional training seminars, where no one expects to run into teenagers. Because their presence is unexpected, teens are often given more attention and opportunity and can grow from the content as much or more than the intended audience.

Seminars on entrepreneurship, social media management, website development, real estate investment, leadership, and investing are widely available and open to the general public. When I have taken one of my teens to meetings like these, everyone seems to notice them and often want to meet them. Anytime one of the "kids" asks a question, it is taken seriously and answered in a way everyone in the room can understand.

Once, my oldest child had the chance to speak with an internationally known real estate investor at a book-signing table, and I found he could get away with asking questions about what tools the investor used to manage his email, schedule his day, and manage his contacts. The gentleman did not appear to be at all bothered by the inquiries but, rather, seemed to appreciate a sixteen-year-old asking him to share some of his "tricks of the trade." Others nearby frantically scribbled down the wisdom my son was acquiring as a matter of simple, casual conversation with a famous man.

What I have observed from other teens I have encountered in similar situations is they're open to implementing the ideas of experts without hesitation. It still blows my mind when I see teens owning and operating successful businesses and investing wisely, but I have seen it repeatedly. Kids are fearless, and they are able to make good decisions when given good guidance.

Life Direction

"What do you want to be when you grow up?" We have all heard and asked this question many times. But it's the wrong question! Indeed, there is much wrong with the question. It implies that a job defines you as a person. It implies that you are nothing until you get that job. It implies that adulthood is an end point, a destination, a finish line. Most people ask this question without meaning to convey any of these messages. Yet so many have bought into the messages hidden in the question.

Parents should be helping their children discover the gifts, abilities, interests, and passions that will guide them to places where they can make an impact. As Jan and I watched our children develop, we discovered how little effect we had on which skills and talents they possessed or what motivated them. Each of the children was a unique package that we had to unwrap layer by layer to discover who they were and where they fit in this world. Some were clearly inclined toward art, others toward analysis; some were detail-oriented, others chaotic; some were passionate, others were cautious; some were competitive, others were compassionate. Each was a unique blend well suited to some fields but not others. As their parents, it was our job to help them know themselves and find an impactful role that was a good fit.

Earlier, I intimated how we had been guilty at times of hoping one of the children would accomplish something we had failed to succeed in doing ourselves, but we eventually realized our purpose as parents was best accomplished by working as a guide or coach rather than a commander. Successful coaches put their team together based on the unique skills of the players, placing them where they can be most successful and have the greatest impact. The coach first studies his players' talents and strengths before assigning them a position, and then he studies them as they play the position to see if they truly fit there. When a coach gets locked into forcing a player to play the wrong position, everyone around them seems to suffer.

Likewise, as a parent, it's a dangerous proposition to predetermine what our children will become and focus all our energies on pushing them to follow that path. There is much good in exposing them to a field you think might be good for them, and where they would likely find success. But we have all seen or read of parents who have forced their own vision on a child with tragic results.

If they are available to you, aptitude and personality testing can be tools to help you guide your teen as he considers his life options. A friend in Virginia whom I greatly respect had extensive tests performed on all eight of her children to try to understand each one's uniqueness. She tells of how the testing helped her become a guide to her children in their professional development, and how it also helped her understand the choices, actions, and attitudes she was seeing in family interactions.

The test results explained to all why they thought one family member was being apathetic when he was merely prone to consider all his options thoroughly before answering questions or responding to requests. They now expect a delay rather than be aggravated by it, and their new understanding helps prevent tension. Everyone now knows if they have a question that requires a lot of detailed thought, they go to that family member. So you can see that these kinds of tests can help with more than just career choices.

Most people in America who finish college earn degrees for a field they never work in. We all know someone who has. In fact, I'm one of them. I have a degree in chemistry and have never worked in the chemistry field. Though college degrees and advanced studies are often valuable, many people do not need traditional college to fulfill their life purpose. For them, college might be a huge waste of time, money, and emotional energy. Testing and evaluation before college may be helpful to make the right decisions where and *if* to attend. Anything that can help your child discover the direction for his or her life is worth exploring.

The reality of our current culture is that most people change jobs and even switch their field of work several times in their career. With this in mind, consider helping your teen to start simply by gathering some work experience just to get the ball rolling. Short-term jobs can give a teen perspective on future long-term decisions and reduce the stress of having to "get it right" the first time. Part-time or short-term employment can give them bits of insight to narrow the field of options that lay before them. Spending time in a work environment also exposes them to jobs in loosely related fields, even jobs they never knew existed. For example, working as a hotel clerk would introduce them to a payroll clerk, a building maintenance worker, a heating and air conditioning contractor, a pool maintenance or installation service, and of course, professionals from various fields who stay overnight. Working as a stocker in a grocery would expose them to the trucking industry, inventory management, customer service, floor maintenance, and packaging and labeling, to name a few.

Hopefully, you can see how any participation in the work world can help teens overcome "paralysis by analysis" when their choices seem limitless. Even volunteering in the community can help them gain a vision for their future, so consider contacting hospitals, nursing facilities, and elderly services, who all need volunteers. Sailors say, "You cannot steer a ship unless it is moving." Any movement or action, even in the wrong direction, can help young men and women discover their right heading.

CHAPTER 12

Inspiration: Fuel for the Future

A quote often attributed to the Irish poet W. B. Yeats states, "Education is not merely the filling of a pail, but the lighting of a fire." It's often cited when writing about education, but the concept is true about parenting as well. Our job as parents requires that we fan the flame of our children's giftings, interests, and activities so that when they leave the nest, they will feel a fire burning within them as they pursue their life's purpose. Another word for this is *inspiration*.

Inspiration is far different from the training, empowering, and transitioning discussed in earlier chapters. Skill development is great, and helping our children transition from parent-control to self-control is essential. There is power in the inspiration you can provide as you join them in dreaming about their place in the world. Fueling their dreams provides them energy to overcome the fear of failure that attacks a person upon any new endeavor or significant change.

Don't Be a Dream Killer

We've all had dreams of becoming significant or making a real contribution in this world. Most people, however, have their passions extinguished at an early stage by dream killers. In his book *Dream Big— But Beware of Dream Killers*, Todd Wilson describes the many things that kill people's dreams, their hopes, their aspirations. Todd appeals to parents to "not be dream killers" in the lives of their children.[1]

When our children tell us what they want to be or do when they grow up, it's so easy to let pragmatic or practical thinking cause us to list the obstacles to our children's dreams or simply pronounce, "You can't do that," thus killing the dream in its infancy. As parents, we fear their failure more than they do. So we must remember that failure is only certain if no one tries.

My daughter was working in food service in New Orleans. "Food service" is a fancy term for waiting tables in a restaurant. She called me one day to ask my opinion about her starting her own business. For years, she had been making hand-bound journals as a hobby and thought maybe now it was time to turn it into a business. She had a dream of making a living from the thing she loved doing, making specialty journals.

My first thoughts turned to the risks of giving up a regular, predictable paycheck to pursue an uncertainty that also had potential upside. I had to contain my caution and resorted to asking a series of questions.

"How much money do you have to get started?"

"Do you have any clear markets for your product?"

"What would you do if it was a complete flop?"

For each query, she had a plan. She had counted the cost and the risk. She had considered contingency plans yet had clearly in her sights the potential for a life of impact and excitement. While she had been dreaming, she had been also analyzing. I was proud of her willingness to bravely consider such a major life change.

It was my job as her parent and counselor to not kill her dream but, instead, fan the flame of her dream with confidence and inspiration. For her, pulling the trigger was the hard part. She had developed the skills, determined her supply sources, evaluated the potential market, and counted her money. It was getting started that required some inspiration.

This may not sound very inspirational, but I said, "Emily, I don't see what you have to lose, other than all your savings, and you have a plan for dealing with that. You don't have a family depending on your income, and you have shown me that you know how to live on minimal income. I think you should go for it."

Inspiration doesn't have to look like cheerleaders with pom-poms and megaphones stirring up a raucous crowd. It may be as simple as confident assurance voiced in statements like "I believe you can do it!" or "I think you should try." A parent's approval or confidence is often the thing our children need to pull the trigger on a life-changing opportunity. If we have trained them well, if they are aware of their giftings and their weaknesses, they will be equipped to take reasonable risks. Our job now is to help them pursue dreams, to encourage them with "I think you're onto something good."

Perhaps you're thinking that inspiration is still a long way off in your parenting journey, but encouragement is an ever-present need regardless of the child's current age or developmental stage. It's so important to practice inspiring your children while the risks are small, before you're needed to guide them through major life changes like starting a business or choosing a spouse. It's shouting, "You are brave! You can do it! I'm watching" when they're standing at the edge of the swimming pool, fearful of jumping in. It's the encouragement your son needs to enter an art contest, and you say, "I've seen your work, and it is good enough to enter." It's attending a community theater production with your stagestruck daughter and leaning over to whisper in her ear, "I think you would enjoy being in the next play they are producing. Tryouts are in two weeks." These are low-risk efforts to inspire, but they clearly communicate that you believe in their potential.

The Power of Your Praise

The story of Benjamin West, the world-renowned eighteenth-century artist, has inspired me to consider the impact of my words to my children in ordinary life situations. He once said, "I became an artist because my mother believed I was one." He went on to describe an incident in which his mother ran an errand, leaving his sister and him at home to entertain themselves. They busied themselves with play. She got her dolls, and he got out paper and ink to draw a picture. In the process of drawing a picture of his sister playing with her dolls, he spilled the ink, making a mess on the page and the table. When his mother returned, she saw the mess but focused on the drawing, and she said to him, "What a lovely picture! You are such an artist." As she kissed him on the forehead, he beamed with pride. "That day," he later said, "I became an artist."

Imagine the difference it would have made for young Ben if his mother had said, "Look at the mess you have made! What am I going to do with you?" Instead, the affirmation she freely and lovingly offered inspired him to see something she saw in him—a masterpiece, not a mistake.

The words you speak to your children are powerful and can open doors of possibility for them. As you encourage them in their abilities and passions, you're pronouncing for them a belief that they are uniquely gifted for a purpose they must fulfill. Casually spoken words of confidence can sink deep into their souls and provide them the fuel to develop their expertise as a mother's words did for the young artist.

Negative or fearful comments flow so easily from our lips, and we all have had those regretful moments when we said something we would like to take back. Words that inflict pain or espouse defeat have tremendous power, as confirmed by studies comparing the results of negative versus positive remarks. Psychological researcher Dr. John Gottman has determined that it takes five or more positive or affirming remarks to counteract the impact of one negative remark.[2]

Training ourselves to inspire our children begins by planning a positive, hopeful, or affirming remark and then looking for a time to say it. If this is a difficult thing for you, use a quote or the words of others. For those of us who came from homes that were not affirming or inspiring, it can feel unnatural or fake to force positivity, but I can personally attest to the fact it can be done.

Though I didn't have a harsh, negative upbringing, my siblings and I were repeatedly challenged to "do better." My older siblings appear to have endured a much more confrontational upbringing than I did, but none of us had inspiration modeled for us at home. I learned it from books and individuals who taught me the important role that inspiration plays in the growth, development, and behavior of others, especially children.

Look for Opportunities to Praise Your Children

Your children need to experience your pleasure and your approval in ways we touched on in chapter 6, including eye contact, focused attention, and physical touch. These build a sense of security for the child. But your words form the substance of inspiration. We are inspired when the words of others—heard minutes or months ago—remind us that someone we respect believes we are up to the task before us.

"Praise is to children what the sun is to flowers."[3] Penned by nineteenth-century writer Christian Nestell Bovee, these words have guided me, and I hope they inspire you to praise your children for who they are with a view to their impact on the world. It's a privilege to be able to speak into your children's lives, a privilege you must prepare for to achieve the greatest impact. Your children want to know your sincere thoughts and dreams about them, and you need to watch for windows of opportunity to light the fire within.

Opportunities to inspire include both spoken and written words. Writing words to affirm and inspire is a great place to start with an older child who may have not felt your pleasure consistently in the past. Not only does writing your thoughts give you time to think about how to say something, but it will also give your son or daughter the opportunity to re-read your words (after recovering from their surprise). You might write something in a greeting card for a special occasion, but writing affirmations works best when they're not expected. Your child may feel like your words are more sincere if it's not just an obligatory note to mark the occasion. Tucking a card that is blank, except for your message to the child, into a book or their sock drawer for them to find randomly is a nice surprise.

Be Sincere and Be Specific

Praise should be sincere, specific, and non-manipulative to have its full effect.

It's important that the praise you give is not an attempt to get something—even love—from your child. Children are highly perceptive and quick to catch on if the words are not sincere, so be careful to think solely of the child's benefit when offering praise.

Praise should also be specific. The more vague your praise, the less genuine it feels. Make your praise specific to the child and related to the child's actions, attitudes, or attributes. It's not enough to say, "Good job!" or shout, "Attaboy!" or "You are a fine young lady!" General statements such as these are surprisingly neutral, rendering neither positive nor negative impact (though they're better than silence).

Specific praise that serves to inspire and support would be more like, "Great job on weeding that flower bed! You were so diligent and committed to going beyond what was expected. And that made all the difference." Or, "You impressed me with your determination to do the job with excellence. The world needs more people like you." And maybe, "I noticed how nice you were to that lady when you helped her in out of the rain. That sets you apart from the average person. That made me so proud of who you have become."

Do you see the difference in how specific references to actions, attitudes, or demonstrated attributes might inspire the child to continue in this vein? Giving praise that is specific has power not just with your children but also with your spouse, your friends, and co-workers. Everyone appreciates being noticed and recognized for their efforts.

Manipulative praise, on the other hand, is associated with several derogatory phrases: *brown-nosing, blowing smoke, schmoozing, sweet-talking,* and *sucking up,* to name a few. Our praise must be pure in its motive of nourishing our children's dreams and fanning the flames of their own giftings and interests, not our own plans for them. When praising someone to further our own agenda, the praise becomes manipulative and ineffective.

What Gets Pictured, Gets Done

As you come to know the inner person of your child and not just what he is involved in, you will be able to praise the actions, attitudes, and attributes that are essence of who he is. When you do that, your child will feel known, loved, and valued. And that is inspirational.

There are other ways we can inspire our children besides kind words and praises. We can suggest to them possibilities they may not think is within their reach, or have never considered. For instance, Jan often would casually mention to our kids, "One day when you own your own business..." or "When you are leading a group of men..." or "When you are speaking to thousands...you need to keep these things in mind." And she would just keep on doing whatever was occupying her, as if the fantastical situation she mentioned was really going to happen. To our surprise, some of them did. In fact, many of them did.

As I mentioned, our oldest son was involved with 4-H. One day, he expressed a desire to run for the office of state president. When we asked him why he wanted to pursue the office, he replied, "You said I was going to be state president!" He reminded us of the time when he was ten years old and serving as president of our small 4-H club of four families that met in our living room. He was resisting having to learn how to lead the meeting by following the agenda of old business, new business, etc. He wanted to know why he had to do it that way, and Jan explained, "Because when you are the state 4-H president, you will need to know this stuff." And he did become the state president! Was it because his mother put the idea in his head? Or because he believed it was his purpose? Or just because he believed it was possible? I don't know. But I do know that a parent's words about what is possible give children the power and permission to pursue such dreams.

Please understand that pushing a child toward a specific job or career or achievement is not what I am advocating. As a matter of fact, I caution against pushing our children at all. Pushing and inspiring are altogether different. Pushing is an attempt to overcome a lack of desire, whereas inspiring is fanning the flame of desire to help the child overcome obstacles to making the desire a reality. Inspiration is giving children the ability to clearly picture what it would look like to accomplish the necessary milestones to achieving their dreams.

John Maxwell speaks of this when teaching on vision in leadership. He likes to say that what gets pictured, gets done. Thus, the clearer the picture, the greater the chance of accomplishing it. Being able to see a destination or a goal in one's mind helps start his or her movement in that direction. And when the going gets tough, a clear picture of the goal helps the person to maintain forward momentum. So vision provides not only direction but also motivation.

Often, our children need us to cast a vision for them, describing with words the ultimate destination they can passionately pursue. I have found it best not to describe concrete goals but, instead, character goals, such as what it looks like to be noble, responsible, kind, generous, or influential. Your family values should be incorporated into the vision you describe for each child, and each child may envision different ways of living out those values. After all, each one has different gifts, abilities, and passions.

Our job as parents is to encourage them along the way, showing them how they are growing toward the goal, the prize of becoming adults who are worthy of respect and able to impact their corner of the world with their gifts and their character. We can help them see their progress along the journey when the desired end still seems a long way off. We can remind them that failure is not final and a setback is simply an opportunity to find a better route.

The Potential for Greatness

It's so important that you find ways to inspire your children to greatness. Remember, they can be great as a minimum-wage laborer, a retail employee, a professional, a business owner, a mother raising children at home, an artist, a writer, or whatever. A person's position does not determine his or her greatness. Greatness comes from within and effects those around them.

During the early stages of child development, we begin the parenting journey by teaching the external aspects of living while establishing control of the child's outward behavior. But we must quickly move to the place where we give up control in favor of influence, for the ultimate goal is to develop in the child an inner person who can live out self-control. It's this inner person who has the potential for greatness.

When you can look back and see that the shift from control to influence has been completed, you can confidently say, "My job is done."

And to that I say, "Well done!"

APPENDIX A

Open-ended Questions and Conversation Fuel

To build relationships with others, including children, dialog is essential. It must truly be a 2-way conversation where each is responding to the other in meaningful ways that is an expression of true interest. Any attempt here to give helpful conversation starters or extenders are NOT an attempt to manipulate a relationship. Rather let these serve as examples of ways to open the process of communication.

For some, these examples will seem unnecessary because you either have good experience in communication, or it is a natural strength. On the other hand, others may find these to be a lifeline to begin to build bridges between you and another person.

Remember, the concept of open-ended questions includes:

1. They are not able to be answered with a few words.
2. They seek more than facts.
3. They seek the intangibles of thoughts, feelings, hopes, or dreams.
4. They are about the other person in the conversation, not about you.
5. There are no right or wrong answers. They may be revealing, or not.
6. They give an opportunity to accept the person regardless their response to the question.
7. It's no about the question, it's about the building of a bridge.

For pre-school ages:

- Tell me about your drawing.
- You are crying. Tell me about your feelings.
- What did you think would happen?
- What's going to happen now?
- How does your doll feel about this situation?
- How can this be better?
- What would you do if you could do magic (or if you had power)?
- Who is your favorite friend? Why? Should other people be like him/her?
- What was your favorite part about today? (or about our trip, a movie, a story)
- Why do you think they did that?
- How would you feel if _____(name a situation)?

For elementary ages: (who are growing in competence)

- What is a task in our family you want to become yours?
- What would be a cool thing to be able to do?
- What do you like about your favorite friend/teacher/toy?
- Tell me about a favorite memory with _____.
- You seem upset. Tell me about what's going on.
- What can be done to make things better?
- What surprised you in the story?
- I want to understand what you are feeling. Can you describe it to me?
- What is the most important thing you want to do today?
- Why is that your favorite?
- Wouldn't it be cool if_____? (Ask the child to think of things that are really not possible.)
- I know you want XYZ. Can you tell me why that is important to you?

Pre-teens: (who are discovering they have feelings)

> - Who is someone you look up to? Tell me about them.
> - What do you wish was true about you?
> - What do you wish was true about me (or another family member)?
> - Tell me about something you daydream about.
> - How do you feel about what happened today? What would you wish you could change about it?
> - Who makes you feel best about yourself? What does he/she do?
> - Where do feelings come from?
> - What about the world is most confusing (or frustrating) to you?
> - Describe what the most amazing person would be like.
> - If you could buy a gift for someone in our family, who would it be and what would you get them?
> - If you could change your school, what would the improved school be like?

Teens: (who want to be taken seriously)

- What do you think cause him/her to do that?
- What would you do if you were in that situation?
- Tell me something interesting about your friend?
- What in the world needs to be changed?
- Where is one of the most interesting places you know about in the world?
- Do you think people are good for animals?
- What kind of animal would you own if it were possible?
- Tell me about one of your favorite songs? What is it about? What do you like about it?
- Who do you think is a great role model? What do you respect about him/her?
- What would be your dream job while you are young? When you get older?
- What would be a cool vacation?
- Tell me about something that scares you.
- How do you calm yourself down when you need to?
- Tell me about a time when you were proud of yourself.
- Tell of a time when you were proud of someone else in our family.
- What makes people bored? It that true for you?
- What is the most important quality in a teacher? Why?
- What is the most important thing you have learned that is not taught in schools? Why do you think that is?
- Do you think social media helps make/maintain friendships? Why/why not?
- What is something that bugs you in your school/church/neighborhood? What can you do about it?
- What is a favorite memory you have with a friend?
- What is the most challenging part of your life right now?
- What YouTube videos or shows would you recommend I watch?
- What is the best gift you ever received?

APPENDIX B

Recommended Resources

Books

Ross Campbell. *How to Really Love Your Child,* revised and updated. Colorado Springs, CO: David C. Cook, 2015.

Ross Campbell, *Relational Parenting.* Chicago: Moody Press, 2000.

Gary Chapman, *The Five Love Languages.* Chicago: Northfield Publishing, 1992.

Gary Chapman and Ross Campbell, *The Five Love Languages of Children: The Secret to Loving Children Effectively.* Chicago: Northfield Publishing, 2016.

James Dobson, *Bringing Up Boys.* Wheaton, IL: Tyndale House, 2001.

James Dobson. *The New Strong-Willed Child.* Wheaton, IL: Tyndale House, 2004.

Steve and Annette Economides, *The MoneySmart Family System: Teaching Financial Independence to Children of Every Age.* Nashville: Thomas Nelson, 2012.

Emerson Eggerichs, *Love & Respect.* Nashville: Thomas Nelson, 2004.

Kathy Koch, *Screens and Teens: Connecting with Our Kids in a Wireless World.* Chicago: Moody Publishers, 2015.

Todd Wilson, *Dream Big . . . but Beware of Dream Killers.* Familyman Ministries, 2010.

Todd Wilson, *Taming the Techno-Beast: Helping You Understand and Navigate Your Child's Electronic World.* Familyman Ministries, 2009.

Milan and Kay Yerkovich, *How We Love.* Colorado Springs, CO: WaterBrook, 2011.

Hal and Melanie Young, *No Longer Little.* Smithfield, NC: Great Waters Press, 2018.

Websites and Blogs

Dr. Kathy Koch, *Celebrate Kids with Dr. Kathy,* www.celebratekids.com

APPENDIX C
Goal Setting Tool

Child: _____

Age: _____

Year: _____

1. Wisdom (Mental growth, knowledge, information, understanding,)

    a. _____
    b. _____
    c. _____
    d. _____

2. Stature (physical growth or control, strength, skills)

    a. _____
    b. _____
    c. _____
    d. _____

3. Spiritual (inner relationship, emotional, religious, values/character)

    a. _____
    b. _____
    c. _____
    d. _____

4. Social (friends, interaction, communication, events, experiences)

    a. _____
    b. _____
    c. _____
    d. _____

APPENDIX D

Family Car Management Plan

Goal: develop a system that provides reliable automobile for transportation that is maintained and financed with reasonable terms, and trains the users to make good decisions and develop good habits.

Method: Every driver of the car records the mileage and purpose of each use, and pays a usage fee per mile that is determined by the average cost of operation. The account that holds the fees pays for fuel, maintenance, and repairs. The users follow the manufacturers guidelines no maintenance schedule. Every occupant is responsible for removing any item or trash they bring into the car at the end of the day. A mileage log/maintenance record is kept in the car.

Parents' responsibility: provide a reliable, safe, insured automobile, and open a bank account to hold the funds.

Average cost of operation calculation:

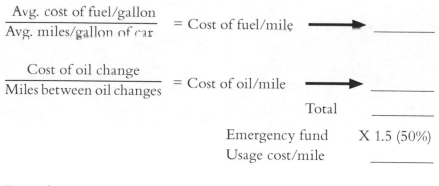

$$\frac{\text{Avg. cost of fuel/gallon}}{\text{Avg. miles/gallon of car}} = \text{Cost of fuel/mile} \longrightarrow \underline{\hspace{2cm}}$$

$$\frac{\text{Cost of oil change}}{\text{Miles between oil changes}} = \text{Cost of oil/mile} \longrightarrow \underline{\hspace{2cm}}$$

Total   _____

Emergency fund   X 1.5 (50%)
Usage cost/mile   _____

Example:

$3.75/gallon ÷ 20 miles/gallon = $0.19/mile
$60/oil change ÷ 3000 miles/change = $0.02/mile

Cost $0.21/mile X 1.5 = 31¢/mile

(Rounding up or down makes it easier)

NOTES

Chapter 1

1 Robert Preidt, "Happiness Might Sometimes Harm Your Heart," *WebMD*, March 3, 2016, www.webmd.com/heart/news/20160303/happiness-might-sometimes-harm-your-heart-study-finds.

Chapter 2

1 Dr. D. Ross Campbell, *How to Really Love Your Child* (Colorado Springs, CO: David C. Cook, 2003), 14.
2 1 John 4:18.

Chapter 5

1 Dr. Brian Ray, "Gen2 Survey," National Home Education Research Institute (Elizabeth, CO: Generations with Vision, 2015).

Chapter 6

1 John C. Maxwell, *The 21 Irrefutable Laws of Leadership: 10ᵗʰ Anniversary Edition* (Nashville: Thomas Nelson, 2007), 25.
2 D. Ross Campbell, *How to Really Love Your Child* (Colorado Springs, CO: David C Cook, 2004).
3 Ashley Groh, et. al, "The Significance of Attachment Security for Children's Social Competence with Peers: A Meta-Analytic Study," *Attachment & Human Development* 16 (2014): 103–136; E. Moss and D. St-Laurent, "Attachment

at School Age and Academic Performance," *Developmental Psychology* 37 (November 2001): 863–874.

4   Ross Campbell, *Relational Parenting* (Chicago: Moody Press, 2000), 16.

Chapter 7

1   Proverbs 27:17.

Chapter 8

1   Proverbs 22:6
2   See Romans 8:18.
3   Ken Blanchard and Spencer Johnson, *The One Minute Manager* (New York: William Morrow, 1982).

Chapter 9

1   Hal and Melanie Young, *No Longer Little* (Smithfield, NC: Great Waters Press, 2018).
2   Dr. James Dobson, *Bringing Up Boys* (Wheaton, IL: Tyndale House, 2001).
3   US Army General Lewis Hershey, www.brainyquote.com/authors/lewis-b-hershey-quotes
4   Stephen R. Covey, *The 7 Habits of Highly Effective People* (New York: Free Press, 1989).

Chapter 10

1   John C. Maxwell, *The 21 Irrefutable Laws of Leadership: 10th Anniversary Edition*, 116.
2   Gary Chapman, *The Five Love Languages* (Chicago: Northfield Publishing, 1992).
3   Quoted by Noah Brooks, "Lincoln's Imagination," *Scribner's Monthly* 18 (August 1879).
4   Dr. Emerson Eggerichs, *Love & Respect* (Nashville: Thomas Nelson, 2004).
5   Milan and Kay Yerkovich, *How We Love* (Colorado Springs, CO: WaterBrook, 2011).

Chapter 11

1   Dr. Kathy Koch, *Screens and Teens: Connecting with Our Kids in a Wireless World* (Chicago: Moody Publishers, 2015).
2   Todd Wilson, *Taming the Techno-Beast: Helping You Understand and Navigate Your Child's Electronic World* (Familyman Ministries, 2009).
3   Steve and Annette Economides, *The MoneySmart Family System: Teaching Financial Independence to Children of Every Age* (Nashville: Thomas Nelson, 2012).

Chapter 12

1   Todd Wilson, *Dream Big—But Beware of Dream Killers* (Familyman Ministries, 2010).
2   Study quoted by Kyle Benson, "The Magic Relationship Ratio, According to Science," *The Gottman Institute*, www.gottman.com/blog/the-magic-relationship-ratio-according-science (accessed Sept. 13, 2021).
3   Christian Nestell Bovee, *Intuitions and Summaries of Thought* (Boston: W. Veazie, 1862).

Printed in the United States
by Baker & Taylor Publisher Services